The Greenhaven
Literary Mover

American
Realism

Christopher Smith, *Book Editor*

David L. Bender, *Publisher*

Bruno Leone, *Executive Editor*

Bonnie Szumski, *Editorial Director*

David M. Haugen, *Managing Editor*

Greenhaven Press, Inc., San Diego, California

Every effort has been made to trace the owners of copyrighted material. The articles in this volume may have been edited for content, length, and/or reading level. The titles have been changed to enhance the editorial purpose. Those interested in locating the original source will find the complete citation on the first page of each article.

Library of Congress Cataloging-in-Publication Data

American realism / Christopher Smith, book editor.
  p.   cm. — (The Greenhaven Press companion to literary movements and genres)
    Includes bibliographical references and index.
    ISBN 0-7377-0323-7 (pbk. : alk. paper) —
ISBN 0-7377-0324-5 (lib. bdg. : alk. paper)
    1. American literature—History and criticism.
2. Naturalism in literature. 3. Realism in literature.
I. Smith, Christopher, 1963–   . II. Series.

PS169.R43 R43   2000
810.9'12—dc21   99-053714
                                                                   CIP

Cover photo: Los Angeles County Museum of Art, detail from "Cliff Dwellers," George Bellows, Copyright ©1998 Museum Associates, Los Angeles County Museum of Art. The complete image can be found on page 208 of this book. All rights reserved.

Copyright ©2000 by Greenhaven Press, Inc.
PO Box 289009
San Diego, CA 92198-9009
Printed in the U.S.A.

CONTENTS

Chapter 1: Defining Realism

Chapter 2: The Rise of Naturalism

Chapter 5: Realism After 1914

FOREWORD

The study of literature most often involves focusing on an individual work and uncovering its themes, stylistic conventions, and historical relevance. It is also enlightening to examine multiple works by a single author, identifying similarities and differences among texts and tracing the author's development as an artist.

While the study of individual works and authors is instructive, however, examining groups of authors who shared certain cultural or historical experiences adds a further richness to the study of literature. By focusing on literary movements and genres, readers gain a greater appreciation of influence of historical events and social circumstances on the development of particular literary forms and themes. For example, in the early twentieth century, rapid technological and industrial advances, mass urban migration, World War I, and other events contributed to the emergence of a movement known as American modernism. The dramatic social changes, and the uncertainty they created, were reflected in an increased use of free verse in poetry, the stream-of-consciousness technique in fiction, and a general sense of historical discontinuity and crisis of faith in most of the literature of the era. By focusing on these commonalities, readers attain a more comprehensive picture of the complex interplay of social, economic, political, aesthetic, and philosophical forces and ideas that create the tenor of any era. In the nineteenth-century American romanticism movement, for example, authors shared many ideas concerning the preeminence of the self-reliant individual, the infusion of nature with spiritual significance, and the potential of persons to achieve transcendence via communion with nature. However, despite their commonalities, American romantics often differed significantly in their thematic and stylistic approaches. Walt Whitman celebrated the communal nature of America's open democratic society, while Ralph Waldo

Emerson expressed the need for individuals to pursue their own fulfillment regardless of their fellow citizens. Herman Melville wrote novels in a largely naturalistic style whereas Nathaniel Hawthorne's novels were gothic and allegorical.

Another valuable reason to investigate literary movements and genres lies in their potential to clarify the process of literary evolution. By examining groups of authors, literary trends across time become evident. The reader learns, for instance, how English romanticism was transformed as it crossed the Atlantic to America. The poetry of Lord Byron, William Wordsworth, and John Keats celebrated the restorative potential of rural scenes. The American romantics, writing later in the century, shared their English counterparts' faith in nature; but American authors were more likely to present an ambiguous view of nature as a source of liberation as well as the dwelling place of personal demons. The whale in Melville's *Moby-Dick* and the forests in Hawthorne's novels and stories bear little resemblance to the benign pastoral scenes in Wordsworth's lyric poems.

Each volume in Greenhaven Press's Companions to Literary Movements and Genres series begins with an introductory essay that places the topic in a historical and literary context. The essays that follow are carefully chosen and edited for ease of comprehension. These essays are arranged into clearly defined chapters that are outlined in a concise annotated table of contents. Finally, a thorough chronology maps out crucial literary milestones of the movement or genre as well as significant social and historical events. Readers will benefit from the structure and coherence that these features lend to material that is often challenging. With Greenhaven's Literary Movements and Genres in hand, readers will be better able to comprehend and appreciate the major literary works and their impact on society.

INTRODUCTION

The years 1865–1914 have come to be known as the Age of Realism in American literature, and Realism in one form or another now stands as one of the most important and enduring movements in American literary history. Although Modernism temporarily displaced it in the 1920s, and Postmodernism continues to call into question its relevance, Realism has continued to exert an enormous influence in the work of major writers and the expectations of modern readers. The first Realist experiments of Mark Twain, William Dean Howells, and Henry James in the 1870s and 1880s were seen as "radical," were often viewed with hostility, and were sometimes surrounded by controversy. Today, the novels of contemporary Realists such as Saul Bellow, Joyce Carol Oates, Anne Tyler, and John Updike are both critically acclaimed and commercially successful. The vigorous continuation of a movement set in motion in America over 130 years ago attests to the durability and continuing relevance of Realism in both American literature and American life.

Realism assumes a commonly shared approach toward what constitutes the "realistic" in life and literature. Readers of science fiction or fantasy novels expect to be transported into worlds far removed from their own. However, when a novel sets out to imitate familiar experiences and places, readers often judge its success by how closely it conforms to standards of "reality" they have subconsciously set for it. Plots and characters that manage to *expand* the bounds of the probable serve to enrich readers' sense of themselves as individuals and heighten their sense of the social environment. However, a novel will fail if it lapses into an overly neat, strained, or stereotypical ending, or if the characters act in a way that is at odds with how readers would expect either themselves or other people to act in a similar situation. Credibility is central to the task of Realism, and readers have come to expect it from certain novels they read and films they see. So embedded have these expectations become, that in retrospect it is hard to believe that, for a long time, many of America's greatest nineteenth-century novelists were at best misunderstood, and at worst banned, for attempting to reflect and explore everyday life.

Realism nonetheless moved steadily from the margins of American culture into the mainstream because it made such a valiant attempt to come to terms with the staggering changes that took place in American life in the aftermath of the Civil War. Few Realists ever claimed to have the right answers for what ailed American society. However, in a time of great anxiety and uncertainty, the Realists elevated the status of the novel by at least asking the right questions. For the first time, if literature was to be seen as "serious," it was expected to offer an engagement with the real world rather than an escape from it. Therefore, it is no surprise that Realism examines with tremendous depth and subtlety so many of the issues that perplexed Americans then and continue to do so now: the implications of scientific advances and modernization; the growth of cities and the corresponding decline of rural communities; the struggle for women's rights; tensions arising from immigration and race relations; and the painful transformation of family life.

True to the conflicted nature of the time, throughout the 1880s and 1890s the Realists debated the definition of Realism, what it should try to achieve, and how it should represent itself in criticism and in literature. Debates about the successes and failures of Realism surfaced almost as soon as the movement began, and these debates continue to this day. Drawing on the work of some of the most considerable scholars of American literature from the last fifty years, *American Realism* illuminates the complexity of this crucial time in the nation's literary history, and the extent to which Realism spoke to its own time and continues to speak to today's world.

A HISTORICAL OVERVIEW
OF AMERICAN REALISM

Accounts of America's cultural history uniformly agree that the best, most enduring literature produced in the period between the end of the Civil War in 1865 and the beginning of World War I in 1914 falls under the broad category of Realism. Critics and historians agree that the struggles and sacrifices necessary to end slavery and unify the nation radically transformed Americans' views of themselves, their society, and the world at large. Consequently, Romanticism's obscure yearnings and Sentimentalism's overly emotional distortions of reality—which dominated the literature of the 1840s and 1850s—could no longer adequately communicate the new challenges confronting the nation. Throughout the 1870s and 1880s, Realist writers and reviewers—committed to the "aesthetic of the common," as William Dean Howells once defined Realism—increasingly dominated debates over the nature and purpose of American literature. Just as Realism ascended at the end of the Civil War, so too did it decline somewhat with the onset of World War I. The Great War destroyed nineteenth-century assumptions regarding the inevitable progress and superiority of Western civilization. Once again literature was transformed to meet the anxieties and new cultural needs of Europe and America. Realism came to be viewed as a somewhat outmoded form of expression, belonging to a bygone era, and all that was new and interesting in literature was seen as emanating from a more radical movement, Modernism. Thus the Age of Realism came to an end; the period spanning the years 1865 to 1914 has since presented itself as a literary and artistic period worthy of in-depth, specialized study.

Such sweeping overviews of American literary history do serve as a useful approach to the subject, but also tend to oversimplify matters and should be applied with caution. Just as traces of Romanticism remained in many of the Realists, so too did Modernism reconfigure Realism for its own purposes rather than rejecting it out of hand. In retrospect, Realism never truly lost its hold on twentieth-century American literature. Moreover, on closer inspection, the movement itself encompasses significant variety and prompts important questions. How, for instance, does one reconcile the work of Henry James with that of Mark Twain? Can Naturalism be viewed as a literary genre fundamentally aligned to the principles of Realism, or as a distinct literary phenomenon? Where too does one place the impressive amount of regional or local color literature written in this period, and how does one account for the increasingly complex exploration of women's rights and race issues that Realism allowed?

All in all, it is more accurate to identify not one Realism, but a number of "Realisms." However, the range of competing voices that fall under the broad category of Realism should not be seen as a barrier to understanding the literature produced in America in the late nineteenth and early twentieth centuries. Rather, it is rewarding to see this tremendous range of literary production as a rich and complex response to the hopes and fears that accompanied American life in this period. Critic Donald Pizer maintains that American Realism, in a significant departure from its European counterpart, has been defined by "a substitution of historical event for ideology as the significant basis for understanding literary production." By this, Pizer means that the relative lack of a coherent philosophy and unity among the Realists means that definitions of American Realism are time-bound by the decades between the Civil War and World War I, rather than framed by a clear philosophy. Though Howells, Henry James, and later Hamlin Garland and Frank Norris did develop coherent if rather uneven ideas regarding how Realist and Naturalist literature should be written, there is some merit to Pizer's contention. Therefore it is crucial that, before we see how authors and critics attempted to define Realism, we understand the events that both defined Realism and fueled Realism's complex interaction with history and change.

The End of the Civil War

There have been many watershed episodes in American history, from the signing of the Declaration of Independence to the Watergate scandal of the 1970s. Without a doubt, the Civil War (1861–1865) was a pivotal event; there is no question that America was significantly altered by this cataclysmic conflict. Communities were torn apart or completely destroyed, and few families escaped the staggering toll of 600,000 lives lost. There were larger implications: Before the Civil War, America was not a nation in the sense we know it today, but rather a loose collection of states, united if at all by their respective positions on slavery. With slavery's defeat, the North's economic model of individual enterprise and industrial modernization asserted its supremacy throughout America. The postwar era known as Reconstruction, from 1865–1877, was an attempt—much resented and resisted in the South—to impose northern social, economic, and political models on the nation as a whole. While historians disagree over the success of Reconstruction, there is no question that national unity became more important than states' rights. In the wake of the Civil War, attention turned to what the United States could or would become as a nation.

American Realists thoroughly examined the economic and psychological effects of the Civil War and the changes introduced in the decades that followed; however, the war itself was rarely dealt with directly by the first generation of Realists, despite the fact that they reached intellectual maturity in the 1860s. This surprising omission can possibly be understood best through Henry James's comment, "When history is so hard at work, fiction has little left to say." With the exception of John De Forest's *Miss Ravenal's Conversion* (1867), the only significant Civil War fiction to emerge between 1865 and 1914 was written by Stephen Crane, who was born in 1871, six years after the war ended. The Realists seemed content, like the nation at large, to move forward and confront the questions that arose out of the Civil War, rather than the Civil War itself.

THE RISE OF THE GILDED AGE

The Civil War changed American social and economic life in a number of significant and lasting ways. The War hastened the industrialization of the northern United States, and thus positioned the entire country for a period of sustained peacetime expansion. It was the age of inventions and staggering productivity. Steel production increased 1000 percent between 1870 and 1900, while the invention of the telephone and the electric light fundamentally altered the way people communicated with each other and the manner in which they lived. An important consequence of northern industrialization during the Civil War was the creation of an enormously wealthy class of industrialists who had grown rich on war contracts. Unfortunately, all too often these contracts had been granted through bribes and questionable connections to the federal government. With the end of the war, this class and a horde of attendant opportunists moved to extend their corrupt business practices into the peacetime economy. Thus, the so-called Gilded Age was born. The phrase was taken from the novel of the same name by Mark Twain and Charles Dudley Warner. It signified an age entirely given over to questionable business ethics, the single-minded pursuit and blatant display of wealth, and a government seemingly indifferent to, if not actually implicated in, exploitation of the nation's resources. Quickly there arose in America a class of fabulously wealthy industrialists who came to be known as robber barons. These men—Jay Gould, John D. Rockefeller, Andrew Carnegie, and William Vanderbilt were the most notorious—monopolized America's oil production, steel industry, and railways and ruthlessly quashed competition and labor demands to maximize their profits. The new power and wealth in the nation was increasingly concentrated in fewer hands, and was enjoyed by a few at the expense of many. The gap between a tiny yet enormously wealthy upper class and an ever-expanding working class became wider than ever in the Gilded Age.

The cult of wealth and success was a topic the Realists turned to time and again in their novels and stories. One of Howells's best-known characters is Silas Lapham, a humble Vermont farmer who becomes a millionaire when he discovers a unique mineral composition on his farm that produces a famous brand of paint. Yet he almost loses his family and his soul in the process of becoming so fabulously wealthy. Mark Twain, himself a victim of the desire to "get rich quick," constantly mocked the human desire to sacrifice happiness for the dream of boundless riches, especially in his stories "The Man That Corrupted Hadleyburg" and "The $30,000 Bequest." Wealth, power, and their consequences were fixations of the second generation of Realists, as well. In his novels *McTeague* and *The Pit*, Frank Norris illustrates the connection between greed and humans' most primitive desires. Edith Wharton, herself a member of New York's aristocracy, saw the desire to either have money or keep others from having it as one of the primary sources of human unhappiness. Despite the diversity of their approaches, the Realists were all deeply engaged in recording the contradictions and cruelties of an age in which money defined personality and social behavior.

TERRITORIAL EXPANSION

While the Northeast industrialized, and the agricultural and plantation economy of the South was in the process of being "reconstructed," the end of the Civil War allowed the nation to turn its attention to settling the vast territories west of the Mississippi River. This process had slowed dramatically during the 1850s as the North and South drifted toward civil war, but the subjugation of the Native Americans in the western territories and their removal from tribal lands began in earnest in the 1870s. By the 1880s, the greater part of the western United States had been transformed by mining operations, ranching ventures, and farming settlements. White settlers and politicians became increasingly disinterested in the plight of Native Americans, eventually seeing the forced integration of tribes into so-called civilized society as the only possible resolution to the problem.

Accompanying industrialization, the postwar development of an extensive national network of railways had a tremendous impact on the settlement of the western territories. Towns and farms were quickly established along rail routes, thus establishing a national market for both goods manufactured in the cities and farm products to feed the rapidly growing urban population. With the completion of the transcontinental railroad in 1869, the concept of a nation spanning the continent from the Atlantic to the Pacific entered the national imagination for the first time. Increasingly, the diverse states of America were reconceived in the public imagination as parts of a fully unified, ever-expanding nation with almost limitless potential.

Willa Cather, the most significant fictional chronicler of the nation's prairie settlements, did not turn her attention to community making in the West until *O Pioneers!* (1913), but many other popular novels created images of the cowboy, one of the most important figures in the American imagination. Mark Twain and Bret Harte wrote both travel accounts and fiction of the West in the 1870s, but it was novels such as Owen Wister's *The Virginian* (1902) and Zane Grey's *Riders of the Purple Sage* (1912) that captured the public's imagination. These best-sellers created an impression of a wild, sometimes violent and lawless West, and reinforced eastern fantasies of frontier individualism and opportunity as the East became increasingly populated, urbanized and industrialized. Settlement of the western territories occurred so rapidly that by the 1890s the frontier was seen as closed, and the United States began to turn its attention to acquiring influence and territory overseas.

THE PAIN OF CHANGE

The image of European immigrants or uprooted Americans advancing westward to found families, farms, and communities in the wilderness is central to the national imagination and the idea of the American Dream. Yet it is also something of a myth. While it is true that there was no shortage of settlers prepared to try their luck out West, most immigrants arrived at and remained in cities, drawn by the ready availability of low-paying, unskilled jobs. Immigration, which had been slow and steady before the Civil War, skyrocketed after 1865. Two and a half million immigrants arrived in the 1870s, and over five million in the 1880s. This influx led to explosive tensions in the nation's larger cities, exacerbated by the fact that America's immigrant base was moving further and further from its Anglo-Saxon roots. Immigrants from countries as diverse as Italy, Greece, and Poland were viewed with both hostility and fear, and American cities became polarized not only by wealth and social status, but by race and ethnicity.

The rise of the role of cities in national life perplexed the many Americans who had grown up in the predominantly agricultural society that characterized the country until the Civil War. Former mercantile centers such as New York and Philadelphia, and frontier towns such as Chicago, were rapidly transformed into modern metropolises whose energy and embrace of modernity increasingly defined the age. Like the nation itself, Realist responses to the specter of the city ranged from awe and amazement to fascination and horror. Howells tried to come to terms with modern New York—with all its poverty, explosive class tensions, and rootless new arrivals—in his novel *A Hazard of New Fortunes*. Theodore Dreiser's *Sister Carrie* begins with the young and naively hopeful Carrie in search of wealth and opportunity. Significantly, though, she is on a train bound not for the wide-open western territories, but for Chicago. Carrie's decision to move from a small town in Indiana to an urban center reflects a larger trend in late-nineteenth-century America.

The major impetus for this demographic shift from farm to city was that plummeting prices for crops had driven rural areas into a sustained period of economic depression and decline in the 1880s and 1890s. The enormous wealth generated by industrialization and the Gilded Age was confined by and large to the cities and manufacturing centers of America. This fact of economic life in Gilded Age America led to deep and lasting divisions between cities and poverty-stricken rural areas. Farmers suffered immense and lasting hardships, weighed down by high transportation costs and crushing mortgages on their land. The plight of farmers and rural areas was largely ignored until the end of the century, when the Populists tried to gain the kind of political representation necessary to address rural needs. However, the tragic impact of modernization and the new culture of money and rampant speculation on rural values was movingly chronicled in the novels and short stories of Hamlin Garland. Having grown up in rather desperate circumstances in the Midwest, Garland knew the life he wrote about. Stories such as "Under the Lion's Paw" and "Up the Coule" dramatically illustrate the simple yet noble aspirations of farmers, and the extent to which they were undermined by ruthless land speculators and American urban culture's indifference to their plight.

The exodus of entire families from the land and into manufacturing and industrial centers unprepared for the influx had far-reaching consequences. Slum housing, crime, and the segmentation of cities into immigrant ghettos, middle-class suburbs, and exclusive neighborhoods for the fashionably rich became facts of urban life. America's cities—as they developed in the wake of industrialization, conflicts between capital and labor, and a hardened class structure—came to especially fascinate the Realists and, later, the Naturalists. In every conceivable way, cities seemed to perfectly embody the Darwinian idea of existence as a savage, purposeless struggle for survival, in which the strongest and most adaptable survived while the weak and indecisive went under. Suddenly it seemed no great imaginative leap for the Naturalists to link the drama of the city to struggles and hierarchies of the primitive jungle that civilization confidently believed it had evolved away from. Three classic works of early American Naturalism—Stephen Crane's *Maggie* (1893), Frank Norris's *McTeague* (1899), and Theodore Dreiser's *Sister Carrie* (1900)—all take the city as their setting, whether it is New York's crime-ridden Bowery, San Francisco, or Dreiser's community of middle-class strivers in Chicago and New York. The Naturalists' creation of the awe-inspiring and terrifying energy and power of the city, often conveyed in transcendent, supremely poetic passages that contrasted with the grim realities of their characters' lives, turned the city itself into a character.

The pace of change, exemplified by the power of money, technological advances, and a reconfiguration of city life, was more than most Americans could comprehend. It is ironic that, just as a newly unified America was in the process of becoming one of the world's most powerful and influential nations, bewilderment, ever-widening social divisions, and a shared anxiety over the future were among the central features of the Age of Realism. One should always approach and explore American Realism with an eye to its attempt to reflect, and make sense of these immense national transformations and contradictions. Of course, inevitable questions arise over what Realism as a theory of writing was, and how it defined itself by strongly opposing other forms of writing current at the time.

WHAT IS REALISM?

Theoretically, a Realist writer engages in what the ancient Greeks called *mimesis*: the imitation, in writing stripped of pretension and artifice, of the people, places, and events that compose contemporary life. A successful Realist writer will illuminate the significance of a way of life that readers often take for granted and customarily dismiss as unimportant. While this sounds like a simple and obvious approach to literary creation, a character from William Dean Howells's classic Realist novel, *The Rise of Silas Lapham* (1885), suggests that this is no easy thing to achieve:

> Commonplace? The commonplace is just that light, impalpable, aerial essence which they've never got into their confounded books yet. The novelist who could interpret the common feelings of commonplace people would have the answer to 'the riddle of the painful earth' on his tongue.

In the nineteenth century, the philosophy of verisimilitude put forward by the Realists led to a rejection of the extreme emotional states and unreal landscapes of Romantic literature, and the impossibly virtuous heroes and heroines of sentimental fiction. Representing the "real" meant that American life and language in all its beauty and ugliness had to be incorporated into a novel. Rather than existing as predictable types, Realist characters reflected the growing interest in psychology, and the recognition that individuals were complex and often driven by contradictory motives. Never before had characters been so fundamental in determining the plot of a novel, and never before had setting, plot, and character worked together so closely to reproduce in fiction the tensions of a society in the midst of such perplexing transformations. The elevation of the commonplace led to the perception of Realism as a radical and sometimes scandalous literary practice. Hitherto ignored topics were suddenly seen as material fit for exploration, and formerly taboo subjects such as divorce, suicide, and adultery—which had always existed but rarely been discussed openly or honestly—were suddenly considered appropriate material for novels.

Having identified some commonly shared preoccupations, a number of questions arise. For instance, Nathaniel Hawthorne's characters often exhibit the kind of psychological complexity and universally identifiable qualities that are associated with Realism. Why then is he considered a writer of romances rather than a Realist? Harriet Beecher Stowe's 1852 best-seller, *Uncle Tom's Cabin*, tackles the most pressing issue of 1850s America—slavery. Therefore, through the medium of her fiction, she was deeply engaged in the social forces and conflicts shaping the nation at the time she was writing. Should Stowe be considered a Realist rather than a Sentimentalist? These questions can best be answered by illustrating how the Realists defined themselves through their rejection of the kinds of literature that preceded them.

REALISM'S REVOLT AGAINST SENTIMENTALITY

No novel better illustrated the power of Sentimentalism in literature than Harriet Beecher Stowe's *Uncle Tom's Cabin*, one of the best-selling novels of the nineteenth century. While it was "realistic" in its willingness to make the cruelty and inhumanity of slavery a subject of debate in the nation, many of the characters were one-dimensional representations of certain positions on slavery, or were broadly sketched types of people affected by slavery. Stowe creates, for example, a profoundly Christian slave, a liberal Northerner, a saintly child, a decadent plantation owner, and a cruel slave overlord, among others. The characters rarely move beyond these static representations, are constantly placed in contrived scenes, and are made to communicate their beliefs and feelings in highly artificial language. However, one cannot deny the widespread effect of the novel's highly emotional scenes on the reading public, and the role the novel played in changing the tide of public opinion regarding slavery. By the 1870s and 1880s, though, the Sentimental novel had degenerated into escapist displays of false, overblown emotions, communicated through an array of predictably stereotyped characters who bore no relation to readers, or anyone else, for that matter. Yet their sales and influence were such that Realists felt obliged to spend a great deal of time and energy criticizing them.

During a dinner party scene in *The Rise of Silas Lapham*, the guests talk about the latest best-selling novel, *Tears, Idle Tears*. As the discussion evolves, it is obvious that this novel is typical of the kind of sentimental fiction the Realists were rebelling against. In the words of one of the characters, "It's perfectly heart-breaking, as you'll imagine from the name; but there's a dear old-fashioned hero and heroine in it who keep dying for each other all the way through and making the most wildly satisfactory and unnecessary sacrifices for each other." *Tears, Idle Tears* is obviously a smash hit, but Howells's objection to it is that it creates a patently false view of life. In the course of the conversation, a Mr. Sewall proclaims that the skewed vision of life these novels offer "do greater mischief than ever." When he goes on to assert that "the novelists might be the greatest possible help to us if they painted life as it is, and human feelings in their true proportion and relation," he is essentially mirroring the philosophy of Howells and many of the American Realists. While one might quite rightly ask for some kind of definition of "life as it is," the idea of portraying "human feelings in their true proportion and relation" is key to the task of the Realists. It reflects perfectly their desire to portray human thoughts and interaction in a recognizable style, and within a credible moral and emotional framework.

One can also see the intensity of the Realists' opposition

to sentimental culture and its effect on the national consciousness in Mark Twain's works. Twain focused his distaste for the sentimental novel on one of its most popular variations, the historical romances of novelists such as Sir Walter Scott. A native of the old South, Mark Twain would later write that the popularity of Sir Walter Scott's novels— with their inflated ideas of chivalry and honor, and their nostalgia for the heroism of times long past—contributed more than anything to the South's willingness to enter into the disastrous Civil War. In *Adventures of Huckleberry Finn* (1884), the Shepherdsons and the Grangerfords are engaged in a bloody, senseless feud over a point of honor that no one can quite remember, yet the slaughter continues. If the Grangerford men are caught in a cycle of meaningless violence in the name of honor, the women complete the family's imitation of Sir Walter Scott's values by celebrating the sentimental cult of lost love and a fixation with death due to a broken heart.

Twain saved his greatest contempt for the novels of "the American Scott," James Fenimore Cooper. According to Twain, Cooper's novels lack structure, in-depth characters who talk like we expect people to talk, and even a smattering of believable scenes. Twain singles out Cooper's *The Deerslayer* (1841) for some of his most hilarious and damning criticism:

> I may be mistaken, but it does seem to me that *Deerslayer* is not a work of art in any sense; it does seem to me that it is destitute of every detail that goes to the making of a work of art; in truth, it seems to me that *Deerslayer* is a literary delerium tremens. . . . Its humor is pathetic, its pathos is funny; its conversations are—oh! indescribable; its love scenes odious; its English a crime against the language.

More than anything, the Realists felt that literature had a moral obligation to present life in all its complex and often ambiguous forms. Therefore, the extreme idealizations of Sentimentalism and the outworn Romanticism of Scott and Cooper were in some ways immoral, since they advocated a patently false view of the world.

REALISM'S DEPARTURE FROM THE ROMANCE

While sentimental fiction was enormously successful and influential in the 1850s, another form of fiction established itself as a unique product of the American environment at this time—the romance. Nathaniel Hawthorne and Herman Melville were the greatest practitioners of the romance in America; typically their works feature characters that represent extreme psychological states or conditions and plots that carry profound symbolic or allegorical overtones. The setting of a romance is usually an equally extreme but again symbolically rich location that often mirrors a character's inner condition. Hawthorne stated in his preface to his novel *The House of the Seven Gables* (1851) that the romance is a genre in which the author can take license with "facts." Therefore, in Melville's *Moby Dick* (1851), the unlikely scenario of Captain Ahab's ship, the *Pequod*, venturing over the entire Atlantic and Pacific Oceans and somehow finding one particular whale is perfectly acceptable within the context of the romance. Hawthorne also stated, however, that though an author might manipulate setting, character, and plot for symbolic and psychological effect, he or she must always remain faithful to the truths of the human heart. By this he meant that the deeper psychological and universal truths must remain intact, even if they are expressed through extraordinary characters and events. Obviously the deeply serious nature of the American Romantics and their achievements had to be taken into account by the Realists. Howells expressed his admiration for the romance, but it was Henry James who wrote the best Realist response to the romance in his 1879 book on Nathaniel Hawthorne.

In this work, James praised Hawthorne's grasp of "the whole deep mystery of man's soul and conscience," as well as his penetrating analysis of New England's moral and political history. However, like many writers who attempt to define themselves by rejecting those who have come before them, James attacks Hawthorne on several fronts. He begins by criticizing the sometimes heavy-handed use of allegory in Hawthorne's short stories, which often led to rather predictable plots and overly obvious moralizing. James praises Hawthorne's greatest work, *The Scarlet Letter*, as a work that possesses "the inexhaustible charm and mystery of great works of art." Yet he also finds shortcomings in the novel's plot, characters, and symbolism, perceiving

> a want of reality and an abuse of the fanciful element—of a certain superficial symbolism. The people strike me not as characters, but as representatives, very picturesquely arranged, of a single state of mind; and the interest of the story lies, not in

them, but in the situation. . . . There is a great deal of symbolism. . . . It is overdone at times, and becomes mechanical.

James was a brilliant critic, and his analysis of Hawthorne
remains by far the best written in the nineteenth century.
However, his criticism reveals as much about himself and
the goals of Realism as it does about Hawthorne's fiction.
Hawthorne's faults in James's eyes—one-dimensional characters, overuse of symbolism, and allegorical plots—had to
be rejected because they diverged significantly from the
complex characters, the everyday, recognizable settings, and
the less sensational yet equally significant plots that characterized Realist fiction. Just as the Realists rejected the
patently false vision of life portrayed in Sentimental fiction,
they also felt an obligation to distinguish themselves from
the psychologically rich, powerfully symbolic, yet not entirely "real" visions of the great romance writers.

THE INFLUENCE OF WILLIAM DEAN HOWELLS

The 1870s and 1880s marked the high point of American Realism, decades dominated by the fiction and criticism of
William Dean Howells, Mark Twain, and Henry James.
These writers constitute the core of the first generation of
American Realists, and they also illustrate the sheer variety
of American Realism. Although he is considered the lesser
novelist of the three, in his day Howells stood at the apex of
this literary triangle. Howells was a very good friend of both
Twain and James, and throughout the 1870s and 1880s, he
used his considerable influence as the editor of the *Atlantic
Monthly* and later *Harper's Monthly* to publish and praise
their work. It was also Howells who, in his position as editor, attacked the excesses of Sentimentalism and Romanticism, and propounded most eloquently the philosophy and
virtues of Realism. He has been called the "middleman" of
culture during the post–Civil War period; through Howells,
Realism moved into the American mainstream. Not only did
Howells support his friends Twain and James, but his infal-
lible knack for recognizing young American writing talent
led to his encouraging and publishing Realist writers such
as William De Forest, Hamlin Garland, Mary Wilkins Freeman, Charles Chesnutt, and Sarah Orne Jewett, to name a
few. Even the younger Naturalist writers such as Stephen
Crane and Frank Norris, who disagreed with Howells's philosophy of literature, were encouraged, favorably reviewed,

and published by him. Although Howells's creative powers and influence declined considerably in first decade of the twentieth century, his importance in advancing American Realism and American literature as a whole in the years 1870 to 1900 cannot be overstated.

As a Realist who sought to reflect the surfaces and depths of American life, Howells often struggled to reconcile his hopes for American democracy with the complex realities of the Gilded Age. He stated in his criticism that the Realist writer "feels in every nerve the equality of things and the unity of men; his soul is exalted, not by vain shows and shadows and ideals, but by realities, in which alone the truth works." In his best work, such as *The Rise of Silas Lapham* and *A Hazard of New Fortunes* (1890), he tried to come to terms with the new culture of money and corruption, as well as the class inequalities that accompanied it. Yet as the 1880s progressed, Howells became increasingly skeptical of the progress of American society, undergoing a crisis of faith in American democracy that led to his public embrace of socialism.

At all times in Howells's fiction, we see the assertion of his ideal of a "fidelity to experience and probability of motive [that] are essential conditions of great literature." One of the most fascinating aspects of his novels is the extent to which all the underlying tensions of the Gilded Age find their way into his characters and the plots in which he frames them. If sometimes the endings of Howells's novels are unsatisfactory, it is because resolving his plots was often as complex as resolving the complexities and contradictions of a rapidly modernizing American society. The problem of satisfactorily incorporating and synthesizing the realities of American life in one of its most complex historical periods was not limited to Howells alone. His great contemporary Mark Twain, who was in many ways a spectacularly representative nineteenth-century American, also had difficulties—albeit different difficulties—in reconciling his fictions of American life with the nation's realities.

MARK TWAIN'S SATIRICAL REALISM

Mark Twain lived through, participated in, and closely observed the modernization of America. He grew up in the pre–Civil War, pre-industrial South, and worked as a riverboat pilot on the Mississippi. After a very brief spell in the Confederate army, he explored the West, working as a prospector and later as a journalist in both Nevada and San Francisco. He gained fame as a speaker, journalist, and travel writer in the late 1860s and early 1870s, and then settled in Hartford, Connecticut. Despite his enormous success, Twain's novels, short stories, and essays show the inner workings of a man who became increasingly skeptical of the price of progress and the pursuit of wealth in America. As his career developed, he turned increasingly to the South of his past for inspiration, or to fablelike but often disturbing short stories of the American present or the very distant European past. Ironically, he pursued wealth with an avidity and single-mindedness that eloquently reflected the period to which his 1873 novel *The Gilded Age* gave its name. For much of his adult life Twain prospered, but he was later bankrupted by the culture of speculation that he both despised and wanted to be a part of. He managed to recoup his fortune, but by 1910, having outlived his wife and children, he died an embittered man. His best work, written in the 1870s and 1880s, illustrates his conflicted and often irreconcilable attitude toward the age in which he lived. One difficulty in reading Twain is that, because he craved success and had a tendency to want to please rather than disturb his readership, he often masked his more incisive comments on what he saw as the injustices and hypocrisy of American life with humor and satire. It is also no accident that, although he constantly returned to the past in his greatest novels—*Adventures of Huckleberry Finn, A Connecticut Yankee in King Arthur's Court* (1889), and *Pudd'n head Wilson* (1894)—he was increasingly confronting the problems facing America in the present.

Twain's originality and the unique nature of his genius set him apart from all other Realists, but *Adventures of Huckleberry Finn* is perhaps the triumph of American Realism. The novel represented, and continues to represent, an enormous expansion of the possibilities of the American novel. The story of Huck's adventures achieves something entirely new through its method of narration and technique. There is no narrator controlling the reader's response to the characters and action, since everything is mediated through the eyes, ears, and voice of Huckleberry Finn. As Twain's biographer Justin Kaplan notes, "Many early readers found Mark Twain's great novel objectionable because it violated genteel standards of literary and social decorum. Instead of refined language, an exemplary hero, and an elevating moral they encountered a narrative written in the idiom of a shiftless, unlettered boy from the lowest class of Southern white society." Suddenly a character's unmediated thoughts and feelings, expressed in the kind of language people really used—rather than the language novelists thought they *should* use—was deemed an appropriate means of telling a story. For later American Realists and Modernists such as Willa Cather and Ernest Hemingway, who read and admired Twain's masterpiece, the bar had been raised, and the way in which characters expressed themselves would never be the same again.

HENRY JAMES: THE REFINED REALIST

Interestingly, the third novelist critics associate with the first generation of major American Realists set only three of his novels entirely in America. Henry James was obsessed in his fiction with portraying in all its richness the "international theme," which refers to the interaction between a young, vital yet culturally shallow American culture on the one hand, and a more sophisticated, culturally richer, but somewhat decadent European culture on the other. James always admired American optimism, confidence, and inventiveness, but he lamented the dearth of cultural sophistication in the nation as a whole. The subtle nuances of European culture and its rich literary and artistic tradition led James to live in France, Italy, and England for virtually his entire adult life. James, who knew and befriended the great European Realists Ivan Turgenev, Gustave Flaubert, and Emile Zola, was a tremendously prolific writer of novels, short stories, and criticism. A productive way to look at his significance as a Realist is by examining his work in light of the principles embodied in his major work of criticism, *The Art of Fiction* (1884).

In this essay, James maintained that the novel must represent "the strange, irregular rhythm of life . . . without arrangement." Just as one's life often appears to be determined by random sequences of events with no apparent rationale, so the novel too must strive to replicate and represent life's strangeness and avoid false, stereotypical plots. The endings of James's novels mirror with tremendous subtlety what he referred to as the ongoing drama of the "human spectacle," where nothing of importance is ever resolved easily, if at all. For James, "Experience is never complete; it is . . . the finest silken threads suspended in the chamber of consciousness, and catching every air-borne particle in its tissue."

Therefore, James's novels typically plumb the psychological depths of humanity, and thereby create characters that possess a complex mixture of both admirable qualities and dubious motives. Everything is perfectly balanced, and there is nothing unrealistically extreme about any of his characters, the choices they make, or their reasons for doing so. Some of James's most famous characters—Isabel Archer in *Portrait of a Lady* (1881), Verena Tarrant in *The Bostonians* (1886), and Lambert Strether in *The Ambassadors* (1901)— are forced into making difficult choices that will determine the future course of their lives. Yet James never makes their choices obvious, and he even leaves an obvious choice— such as Verena's decision to marry Basil Ransom in *The Bostonians*—open to question. If the manner in which James resolves or chooses not to resolve the respective fates of his characters goes against the sentimental wishes and romantic expectations that a reader brings to his novels, on closer examination it is true to the complexities and compromises of the human experience.

James felt strongly that the novel was an art form, and therefore must be as consciously crafted as any painting or sculpture, and his own novels certainly reflect this philosophy. Of all the Realists, James's reputation has remained the most secure, despite accusations that the sophisticated and worldly settings in which his characters and plots moved did not truly confront and negotiate the conflicts and contradictions of late-nineteenth-century American life. Yet the depth and complexity of his characters, the nuances of social interaction embedded in his dialogue, and his subtle exploration of the impact of modernization on the individual and social consciousness are deeply satisfying to readers and writers alike.

THE RISE OF REGIONALISM

While William Dean Howells, Mark Twain, and Henry James mapped out their own literary territory in the Northeast, the South, and Europe, respectively, their respective visions as writers were national, and in James's case, international. During the same period in which these giants of American

Realism wrote, a number of writers chose to assert the importance of the nation's diverse regions. Writers such as Hamlin Garland in the Midwest, George Washington Cable and Kate Chopin in the South, Sarah Orne Jewett and Mary Wilkins Freeman in New England, and Bret Harte in the West are all in one way or another considered regionalists.

Before the Civil War, New Englanders had dominated virtually every aspect of American literature. However, as the nation's growing population settled the continent after 1865, literature celebrating the regional diversity of America came to prominence. Regionalism was often a reaction against the economic impact of industrialization and modernization in America after the Civil War. Many regions, especially rural communities, did not benefit from the enormous economic changes that occurred after the Civil War, and Realist writers felt an obligation to communicate this new fact of American life. The rapid spread of railway lines throughout the nation created a national marketplace, and erased the isolation of many regions. Consequently, writers who felt an attachment to their region felt threatened by the growing standardization of American society. Therefore, regionalist writers began to produce a literature that celebrated the unique language, rituals, and other cultural traits of their part of the country. Regionalism also served a kind of nostalgic function: As more and more Americans moved to the city and lost their regional identities, they sought out a literature that reminded them of their lost origins.

The one regionalist who put forward a coherent philosophy of the movement was Hamlin Garland, whose collection of short stories, *Main-Travelled Roads* (1891), exposed the unspeakable poverty and exploitation of small farmers in the Midwest, and asserted the uniqueness and dignity of their way of life. Drawing on an appropriately rural image, Garland declared that great American art, if it is faithful to American conditions, will "rise out of our conditions as naturally as the corn grows." For Garland, Realism and regionalism went hand in hand; consequently, individualized characters whose lives are not distorted by grossly exaggerated plots are quite naturally attached to a setting "based upon truth to certain localities and conditions." With such a commitment to notions of Realism implicit in regionalism, it is not surprising that Howells supported and published so many budding regionalist writers, and that he saw regionalism as one of the most powerful engines of both genuine American literature and the cause of Realism in general.

REALISM, WOMEN'S ISSUES, AND THE PROBLEM OF RACE

The late nineteenth and early twentieth centuries saw a dramatic reconfiguration of the role of women in society. The ideal woman of 1850s culture had been portrayed as pious, submissive, and nurturing, a figure who asserted her personality and gained identity by cultivating domestic perfection. After the Civil War, though, women gained unprecedented access to higher education, and economic expansion after 1865 led to more job opportunities. Whether through the medium of education, work, reform organizations, or women's clubs, there is no question that the Age of Realism coincided with a broad struggle on the part of women to move out of the private and into the public arena. Kate Chopin, Charlotte Perkins Gilman, Mary Wilkins Freeman, and Edith Wharton fully documented the complex challenges facing women. Later novelists such as Willa Cather and Ellen Glasgow further developed the concerns initiated by the first generation of women Realists. All explore the contradictions of a society that both offered and withheld opportunities and freedoms for women. Change was no doubt occurring, but beneath the surface of social change, a prevailing desire on the part of men and traditional institutions to reaffirm male dominance of the public sphere and women's "place" in the home continued to assert itself.

Given the new questions surrounding women's relationships with men, it is not surprising that the institution of marriage is closely scrutinized in the best work of women Realists. Kate Chopin's *The Awakening* (1899) and Charlotte Perkins Gilmans's story "The Yellow Wallpaper" (1892) explore the consequences of marital frustration and the desire to break free of marriage's oppressive expectations. Chopin's heroine ultimately seeks escape from her predicament by drowning herself, while the female narrator of Gilman's story descends into madness. The tragic endings to these narratives tend to suggest that many women held out little hope of reshaping their lives and their roles as women in society, either because the institution of marriage was simply too monolithic to conquer, or because society would not ultimately allow such freedom and independence. The picture painted by women writers was not entirely bleak, however.

Mary Wilkins Freeman's female characters often succeed in asserting their will and in making free choices within their restricted surroundings. Many of Willa Cather's female characters discover true independence and self-realization either by rejecting marriage out of hand or by dictating the terms of their respective marriages. Yet the impressively independent women of Cather's novels are often balanced against women who live frustrated, emotionally thwarted lives within the confines of failed marriages.

While women were perceived as gaining ground—albeit slowly—the African American population that had supposedly been freed to pursue liberty, wealth, and happiness in the new America now seemed victims of a backlash against social and political aspirations on their part. With the end of Reconstruction in 1877, many southern states introduced draconian laws that severely restricted black voting rights, access to education, and land ownership. A more subtle racism exercised in the North led to an equally stifling sense of poverty, a lack of economic and educational opportunities, and despair regarding any kind of progress. Two black reformers and intellectuals—Booker T. Washington and W.E.B. Du Bois, debated the future role of African American culture and its relationship to America. Washington advocated gradualism and uplift through assimilation into and accommodation with white society. Du Bois took a more militant stance through proud assertions of the depth and resilience of black culture, and through demands for immediate civil rights and equal access to educational opportunities.

Writers such as Mark Twain and George Washington Cable explored the psychological and sociological effects of slavery and its aftermath, but like the depiction of women by writers such as Howells and James, their perspective was limited. The major black writers of this time were Frances Harper, Paul Laurence Dunbar, and Charles Chesnutt. All three were in the difficult position of having to make a living from their writing by appealing to a mostly white readership while communicating the racial injustices that were prevalent throughout the nation. Harper appealed to the sentimental dimension of female readers, while Dunbar often masked his stance on issues of race behind popular "dialect" poems and the Romantic tradition of poetry. The most successful black Realist writer is Charles Chesnutt, whose novels and short stories offer complex negotiations of the "color line" and the tragedy and violence that occurs when that line is crossed by either blacks or whites. His novel *The Marrow of Tradition* (1901) is based on the race massacre that erupted in Wilmington, North Carolina, in 1898, and the circumstances surrounding it. By outlining the sources and tragic consequences of racism in perceptive detail, the novel ends with an indirect plea for good will and compassion on both sides, both of which have been plainly lacking throughout the novel. This desire to induce change by appeasing the white readership whose assumptions he challenged shows the difficult position Chesnutt and African American Realists found themselves in at this time in the nation's history.

THE ORIGINS OF NATURALISM

By the end of the 1890s, a younger generation of writers emerged from the shadow of Howells, Twain, and James, and attempted to offer a more radical vision of and explanation for the changes sweeping America. For writers such as Stephen Crane, Theodore Dreiser, and Frank Norris, Howellsian Realism was seen as too soft, too accommodating to middle-class aspirations, and therefore not "realistic" enough. Norris, the one Naturalist who actually published essays that outlined a vision of American Naturalism, saw Howells's novels as possessing little more than "small passions, restricted emotions, dramas of the reception room, tragedies of an afternoon call, crises involving cups of tea." Norris went on to say that Howells's characters were real enough, were indeed ourselves, as long as "we are well behaved and ordinary and bourgeois, so long as we are not adventurous or not rich or not unconventional." For the younger generation of Naturalists, the extraordinary nature of the times in which they lived demanded an extraordinary kind of literature. Drawing on the ideas set forth by French philosopher Auguste Comte, English scientist Charles Darwin, and French novelist Émile Zola, the philosophy of American literary Naturalism was born.

Auguste Comte was important because he was the first modern thinker to see the impact of scientific thinking on society, as it progressively rejected religion and philosophy as ways of explaining existence. Out of Comte's thinking, the modern study of sociology—the "science of society"—was born. Two years after Comte's death in 1857, Charles Darwin established more firmly the scientific explanation for existence in his *On the Origin of the Species* (1859). Darwin argued that all animal and human behavior was determined by biological impulses rather than divinely inspired reason. He characterized the natural world as a constant struggle for survival, and from this vision of a cruel and random world came the principle of natural selection. Natural selection meant only the species that could constantly adapt to change and successfully evolve would survive, while the weaker species would fail to adapt and degenerate. Darwin's controversial findings undermined the biblical explanation for existence, which portrayed God as having created a finished world with fixed hierarchies in nature. Though the phrase "survival of the fittest" is not Darwin's, many thinkers and writers began to view modern society in terms of Darwinian philosophy. Somehow Darwin's theory of natural selection seemed to offer a rationale for the widening disparity between wealthy and successful members of society and the struggling, wretchedly poor underclass.

Zola applied Comte's thinking and Darwin's philosophy to literature in his essay "Le Roman Experimental." In his rejection of the supernatural and his advocacy of fiction that offers a true and objective account of the contemporary world, Zola's vision of the novel differs little from that of the Realists. However, his emphasis on creating fiction in which characters and outcomes are determined by a biological understanding of society and nature is an important departure from the Realists. Zola strongly believed that novelists should think of their fiction as a scientifically controlled experiment, where characters' behaviors are closely observed as they interact with the forces of nature and society. Thus the study of human nature and society became something of a science in itself in a typical Naturalist novel.

THE VARIETIES OF NATURALISM

Overall, American Naturalism can be divided into two camps. First were those writers who emphasized the biological nature of humans and showed them attempting to utilize their instincts to survive in a hostile natural world. These characters are prone to what Dreiser called "chemic compulsions" (Hurstwood in *Sister Carrie*) and what Norris called "the foul stream of hereditary evil" (*McTeague*). In both cases, this irrational, innately primitive impulse leads to the destruction of the character in question. Besides Dreiser's *Sister Carrie* and Norris's *McTeague*, an example of this kind of Naturalism is found in the character Wolf Larsen in Jack London's *The Sea Wolf*. London's allegorical portraits of human and animal struggles, *The Call of the Wild* and *White Fang*, concentrate on how the natural environment determines both human and animal behavior, and won him enormous popularity and acclaim. Both novels are masterly illustrations of the appeal of animal primitivism and the law of "tooth and claw" for nineteenth-century readers, who were all too aware of how close London's depiction of human and animal nature was to the facts of survival in modern America.

Aside from London's achievements, nature's hostility and indifference to human survival is brilliantly illustrated in Stephen Crane's short story "The Open Boat." Cast adrift on the stormy ocean after their boat has been shipwrecked, the characters are all unnamed. Rather, they are known merely by their professions—the captain, the oiler, the correspondent, and the cook. What Crane is doing here is deliberately creating types rather than individualized characters, which was a significant departure from Realism. Stripping the characters of names is apt in the kind of universe Crane evokes, because once they find themselves alone and imperiled on the ocean, the characters are forced to realize their utter insignificance in the face of an indifferent nature:

> When it occurs to a man that nature does not regard him as important, and that she feels she would not maim the universe by disposing of him, he at first wishes to throw bricks at the temple, and he hates deeply the fact that there are no bricks and no temples.

Crane puts forward the idea of the need for individuals to work together to survive in a hostile environment but, as in so much Naturalist fiction, pure chance determines the outcome of this masterly tale. No guiding hand or natural justice decides who lives and who dies, since the querulous, somewhat cowardly cook survives the ordeal while the oiler, who is more than anyone else responsible for guiding the boat to safety, drowns.

The second kind of Naturalism is more common and less "programmatic" in its approach to characters and action. Writers in this camp adopt a "softer" kind of Naturalism, more concerned with humans in their social environment, and present them as products of socioeconomic (rather than natural) forces against which they struggle but can hardly hope to prevail. Examples of this kind of Naturalism can be found in Hamlin Garland's *Main-Travelled Roads*, Stephen Crane's *Maggie*, and Norris's later two novels, *The Octopus* and *The Pit*. The fact that Norris freely adopted both forms of Naturalism in his three novels illustrates the flexibility of the genre, and how it was viewed as a starting point for a novel rather than a rigid form into which characters and action had to be fitted. This strain of Naturalism, because it can be more subtly integrated into a novel's form, was widely adopted and endured well into the twentieth century, largely because the specter of "socioeconomic forces" could take many forms. In Kate Chopin's *The Awakening* and Edith Wharton's *The House of Mirth* (1905), female characters struggle against and are ultimately consumed by a powerful, ultimately unyielding social code that stipulates women must be either nurturing mothers or objects of male desire. Progressive writers such as Upton Sinclair, whose sensational 1906 novel *The Jungle* led to reform of the meatpacking industry, also created a Naturalistic framework within which the injustices of society could be questioned and explored. By creating sympathy for oppressed characters and their struggles against an unjust and terribly powerful social structure, this kind of Naturalism tried to influence readers to agitate for social change. It is not surprising that many of the Naturalists were thoroughly committed to reform and greater equality at all levels of society.

Later in the twentieth century, Naturalism was adopted by the school of Social Realism, which emerged as a response to the Great Depression of the 1930s, and the perceived need to communicate the plight of the poor and effect social change. The forces against which John Steinbeck's characters struggle are greed and the selfish indifference to the suffering of others that greed generates. In Richard Wright's best-selling *Native Son* (1940), African Americans living in the Chicago slums during the depression are depicted as hopelessly pitted against a racist society that defeats and dehumanizes them and starves them of economic opportunities. Even William Faulkner's great Modernist novels, *The Sound and the Fury* (1929) and *Absalom! Absalom!* (1936), fixated as they are on cultural degeneration and decline in the face of relentless historical forces, utilized strains of Naturalism.

REALISM SINCE 1914

Even before the onset of World War I, with all its world-altering consequences for Western civilization, Realism had begun to face challenges to its cultural supremacy. However, until the bewildering aftermath of the Great War, the alternatives to Realism were too obscure, experimental, or radical to enter the mainstream. Before 1918 the challenges confronting Realism were most evident in the visual arts, where the Impressionism of Monet, Pissarro, and Renoir evolved into the dramatic post-Impressionist experiments of Van Gogh and Cézanne, the violent Expressionist works of Edvard Munch, and the Cubism of Picasso and Braque. The movement in the visual arts away from an objective representation of concrete reality, and toward increasing subjectivity and abstraction prepared the way for Modernist experiments in literature after 1918.

Critics and readers now look back on the 1920s as the age of Modernism, which produced the poetry of T.S. Eliot, Ezra Pound, and William Carlos Williams, as well as the novels of William Faulkner and Gertrude Stein. At the time, however, Williams was completely unknown, and Eliot and Pound were read and appreciated only by a cultural élite of fellow writers and critics. In the years leading up to his being awarded the Nobel Prize in literature in 1949, most of William Faulkner's novels went out of print. Ernest Hemingway, one of the great prose Modernists, was indeed popular, but his desire to pare down his prose so that only the most essential elements of the human experience shine forth makes his debt to Realism obvious. Other more popular novelists and poets of the 1920s were experimental, but their experimentation suggested a rearrangement of Realism rather than a deliberate subversion of its underlying principles. Sherwood Anderson, Sinclair Lewis, Willa Cather, F. Scott Fitzgerald, and Robert Frost were well-loved, best-selling novelists and poets in the 1920s, and they all followed in their own way a path that critic Brian Lee has called "non-doctrinal realism." Anderson's interest in modern psychology, Lewis's use of satire, and the blend of Romanticism and closely observed social detail that characterizes the work of Cather and Fitzgerald marked their respective departures from Howellsian Realism and the hard-line Naturalism of Norris and Dreiser. Yet their commitment to protesting certain trends in American culture, and to accurately depicting the everyday life and language of various regional environments, marks them all as Realists. So while Modernism gained the cultural high ground held by élite artists, writers, and critics during the 1920s, Realism never really lost its esteemed place in reading and publishing circles.

Since World War II, Postmodernism, which proclaims that there is no objective reality, and that the desire to reproduce it in literature is merely a fantasy, has moved to the forefront of American literature. Reveling in a world of chaos, oppressively dominant popular culture images, and media saturation, Postmodernist writers have further subjectivized literature, leading to accusations that it is nothing more than self-indulgent trash. Even today, though, many of America's most significant writers—John Updike, Raymond Carver, Richard Ford, and Joyce Carol Oates—draw heavily on the principles of Realism, seeing the everyday world we inhabit as the one true source of the best, most relevant, and most engaging fiction. No matter what the nature of writers' and critics' objections, there is no indication that Realism in American literature is going to go away, or that it will ever relinquish its hold over both writers and the expectations readers bring to literature.

CHAPTER 1

Defining Realism

American
Realism

The Moral and Thematic Concerns of American Realism

Harold H. Kolb Jr.

Despite the fact that Realism is not a strictly defined philosophy, Harold Kolb Jr. finds a certain continuity of thought and purpose in the Realists. For Kolb, the Realists were united in their commitment to producing literature that is representative of common emotions and experiences, and which conveys a moral purpose. In this selection, Kolb also makes an important distinction between Naturalism—a variation on Realism that dominated American literature in the 1890s—and the realism of writers such as Mark Twain, William Dean Howells, and Henry James. Harold H. Kolb Jr. teaches English at the University of Virginia.

The philosophy of American realism, to borrow [philosopher Thomas] Carlyle's term, is "descendental," or, more accurately, nontranscendental. The realists cannot accept supernaturalism, Platonic idealism, and the worlds of spirit. They do not necessarily deny the validity of such worlds; they simply ignore them as unknowable in ordinary human terms and thus irrelevant to ordinary human experience. The American realists agreed with [philosopher] John Stuart Mill's formulation of the utilitarian position in his *Coleridge*:

> We see no ground for believing that anything can be the object of our knowledge except our experience, and what can be inferred from our experience by the analogies of experience itself; nor that there is any idea, feeling or power in the human mind, which, in order to account for it, requires that its origin should be referred to any other source. . . . There is no knowledge *à priori*; no truths cognizable by the mind's inward light, and grounded on intuitive evidence.

Excerpted from *The Illusion of Life: American Realism as a Literary Form*, by Harold H. Kolb Jr. Copyright ©1969 by The Rectors and Visitors of the University of Virginia. Reprinted with permission from the University Press of Virginia.

This unidealized view of human experience has an artistic corollary. The realists believe that the purpose of art, as always, is to instruct and to please—*aut prodesse aut delectare.* But the instruction and the pleasure lie in giving shape to life's meaning by seeing into human experience, rather than seeing through it to spirit, ideal, or godhead. . . . The philosophical aspect of realism, according to [critic] George Becker, held that "life had no meaning, no telic motion, and that man was a creature barely escaped from the level of animal behavior and driven by forces over which he had no control and in which he could discern no purpose." The basic problem here is the common confusion of realism and naturalism. The two movements are related, but they must be kept separate since they have very different attitudes toward human experience and society. In the mid-1880s the realists denied idealism without embracing pessimism; they rejected the affirmations of Longfellow and Tennyson without accepting the environmental web of Frank Norris and Thomas Hardy. In their best work the realists were pragmatic, relativistic, democratic, and experimental. They were not committed to dogmatic theories or fixed formulas, insisting only that fiction be true to life, that it be interesting, that it be honest, that it be the result of a direct impression of life. In 1885, the house of fiction had [as Henry James said] "not one window, but a million."

THE REALISTS' SUBJECT MATTER

The subject matter of the American realists in the 1880s provides another basis for definition, for all writers are defined to some extent by what they write about. The realistic subject matter is derived directly from the realistic philosophy. Subjects are drawn from "our experience, and what can be inferred from our experience by the analogies of experience itself." The realists write about the common, the average, the unextreme, the representative, the probable. They concern themselves with ordinary human lives seen in the context of normal social relationships. They concentrate on what people are rather than what they ought to be, on men rather than Man. Much of the fiction written in the mid-1880s is topical: the Boston reform movement, feminism, the problem of the new American businessman, the European underground revolutionary movement. Most of the fiction deals with recognizable geographic locations—Boston's

Beacon Street; Hannibal, Missouri; Cairo, Illinois; London's Buckingham Palace Road; the Ponte Vecchio in Florence. . . .

The realists' concern with common experience, contemporary issues, and Baedeker topography should not lead us into the trap of discussing realism in terms of photographic portrayal, statistical norms, a one-to-one correspondence with reality, or a slice of life. A slice of life, like a pound of flesh, is a messy affair. Fiction in the mid-1880s is still fictitious, and James, Howells, and Mark Twain do not choose their topics from raw and unrefined experience. The realists' representation of the common experience is ultimately achieved through imaginative realization rather than reportorial or statistical method. James' short tale, "The Real Thing," treats precisely this point. The artist of the story finds that truly genteel Major and Mrs. Monarch are unsatisfactory as models for illustrations of ladies and gentlemen. The drawings of Mrs. Monarch make her seem seven feet tall; the Major is useful only for brawny giants. The real thing, for the puzzled artist, keeps coming out larger than life, and he discovers "an innate preference for the represented subject over the real one: the defect of the real one was so apt to be a lack of representation."

Another qualification concerning the realists' subject matter needs to be made. The common life and the ordinary characters on which the realists presumably depend are, upon close inspection, not so common and ordinary after all. Runaway slaves, millionaires, revolutionary suicides, and princesses (even democratic ones) are somewhat exceptional. And no important character in the fiction of Henry James can be lightly accused of being ordinary. Even Huck Finn is chosen as much for his unique social position as for his common humanity. "His liberties were totally unrestricted," said Mark Twain of Huck's prototype, Tom Blankenship of Hannibal. "He was the only really independent person—boy or man—in the community." It is Huck's unique freedom which makes possible both the narrative structure of the book and its criticism of contemporary life, for his freedom gives him a distance from the community which makes critical perception possible (at least for the reader, through the point of view of the narrator). Floating down the Mississippi on a raft has been seen as the great American experience. How many Americans have ever done it? The realists concern themselves with characters and events which are imaginatively representative of the common experience, even though the characters and events themselves may be somewhat out of the ordinary, outside the range of the statistical norm. . . .

Realistic subject matter does have room for the exceptional, if it is the humanly exceptional (not the superhumanly or subhumanly exceptional, as in romantic and naturalistic writing). . . .

The subject matter of the realists is chosen from a middle ground. They reject the romance of the gutter as well as the romance of the ideal, a point not always clearly recognized. [Journalist and novelist] Charles Dudley Warner, writing in 1883, stated that "it is held to be artistic to look almost altogether upon the shady and the seamy side of life, giving to this view the name of 'realism'; to select the disagreeable, the vicious, the unwholesome." Warner concluded his catalogue of realistic subject matter with an exclamation that must have swayed the lambrequins in nineteenth-century parlors: "And this is called a picture of real life! Heavens!" This common opinion concerning realism can be seen in the eleventh edition of the *Encyclopaedia Britannica*, which defined the realist as one who "describes ugly things and brings out details of an unsavoury sort," a definition epigrammatized by the acid pen of the devil's lexicographer, Ambrose Bierce: "Realism, n. The art of depicting nature as it is seen by toads." George Becker, tracing realism well into the twentieth century, speaks of the subject matter of the "lower social levels," a view supported by Willard Thorp (realistic characters include "servants, laborers, privates in the army, immigrants, derelicts, the lonely ones, prostitutes, inhabitants of the urban slums and the worn-out farms") and James Colvert ("like the realists, Crane chose certain characteristic subjects and themes—slum life, war, prostitution, and alcoholism").

Once again, however, we must separate realism from naturalism. The subject matter in the novels of the mid-1880s represents a *via media* between the castles of the romancers and the slums of the naturalists. The characters are essentially middle class, and the concerns of the novels are, for the most part, middle-class concerns. The realists open new areas of subject matter for fiction, but they do not open all areas. Overt sexuality, for example, was simply not possible in public American literature in the 1880s just as the bikini bathing suit was not possible on public American beaches in the nineteenth century. Even Mark Twain, who relished ribald tales and regretted that he had to modify for public printing the extravagant and gorgeous language of Jim Gillis of Jackass Gulch, spoke of fiction which poured from [French naturalist writer Emile] "Zola's sewer." Howells' portraits of middle-class women and working girls—Marcia Hubbard, Zerrilla Millon Dewey, Statira Dudley, Amanda Grier—seem tame enough today, but they caused a momentous stir in their time. . . .

Howells, of course, did not deal with sexuality or the lowest social levels, but he and the other realists helped to make these subjects possible for later writers. The realistic movement away from idealism, sentimentality, and romance is evolutionary: Statira Dudley and Zerrilla Dewey are a step toward Crane's Maggie and Dreiser's Carrie. The overtones of Lesbianism in *The Bostonians* are muted but unmistakable. Howells and James, while not dealing directly with sex, do shatter the idealistic (yet hypocritical) nineteenth-century feminine pedestal and open up the entire question of the status of women and their relations with men. Romantic novelist Amelia Barr criticized the realists for depicting girls who were not "nice," girls who were frank, high-handed, freethinking, and contemptuous of authority, girls who rode bicycles, played tennis, and rowed boats—"altogether in accord with an epoch that travels . . . sixty miles an hour." Charles Dudley Warner also condemned the realists for their portraits of "the silly and weak-minded woman, the fast and slangy girl, the *intrigante* and the 'shady.'" It must have distressed Warner to find that the issue of the *Atlantic* which carried his condemnation had, as its leading piece, James' three-act dramatic version of *Daisy Miller*. . . .

"Humor," said Mark Twain, "must not professedly teach and it must not professedly preach, but it must do both if it would live forever." Howells and James would agree, and would expand the statement from humor to all fiction, for the ethical content of realistic novels is so essential that it demands a place as an integral part of the definition of realism. The morality of realism has not always been recognized. Nineteenth-century critics attacked *The Rise of Silas Lapham* as "a book whose moral tone was so unpleasantly, so hopelessly bad." The Concord Library Committee stumbled into fame by calling *Adventures of Huckleberry Finn*

A TRULY DEMOCRATIC AMERICAN LITERATURE

William Dean Howells was the best-known and most influential Realist of his time. As an editor, he arranged for the publication of works by established Realists such as Mark Twain and Henry James, as well as younger writers such as Hamlin Garland and Stephen Crane. Howells also published a great deal of widely read criticism that constantly defended Realism's style of writing and choice of subject matter. Responding in 1891 to British poet Matthew Arnold's charge that American culture lacked distinction, Howells celebrated the democratic impulse behind American Realism, as it sought to assert the richness of the everyday in American life.

In fine, I would have our American novelists be as American as they unconsciously can. Matthew Arnold complained that he found no "distinction" in our life, and I would gladly persuade all artists intending greatness in any kind among us that the recognition of the fact pointed out by Mr. Arnold ought to be a source of inspiration to them, and not discouragement. We have been now some hundred years building up a state on the affirmation of the essential equality of men in their rights and duties, and whether we have been right or wrong the gods have taken us at our word, and have responded to us with a civilization in which there is no "distinction" perceptible to the eye that loves and values it. Such beauty and such grandeur as we have is common beauty, common grandeur, or the beauty and grandeur in which the quality of solidarity so prevails that neither distinguishes itself to the disadvantage of anything else. It seems to me that these conditions invite the artist to the study and the appreciation of the common, and to the portrayal in every art of those finer and higher aspects which unite rather than sever humanity, if he would thrive in our new order of things. The talent that is robust enough to front the every-day world and catch the charm of its work-worn, care-worn, brave, kindly face, need not fear the encounter, though it seems terrible to the sort nurtured in the superstition of the romantic, the bizarre, the heroic, the distinguished, as the things alone worthy of painting or carving or writing. The arts must become democratic, and then we shall have the expression of America in art; and the reproach which Mr. Arnold was half right in making us shall have no justice in it any longer; we shall be "distinguished."

Reprinted from William Dean Howells, *Criticism and Fiction and Other Essays* (New York: New York UP, 1959), 66–67.

"rough, coarse, and inelegant . . . the veriest trash" and ban-
ning the book from the library's refined, elegant, and gram-
matical shelves. The Library Committee was not, as is
sometimes thought, simply another isolated manifestation
of Massachusetts contrariness. The committee's opinion
was apparently a majority one, and was seconded by such
diverse publications as the *Arkansaw Traveler* ("Mark
Twain's latest book . . . is vulgar and coarse") and the
Springfield *Republican* (The "moral level [of Twain's books]
is low, and their perusal can not be anything less than
harmful"). . . .

THE MORAL COMPLEXITY OF REALISM

In spite of these criticisms, perceptive readers have long
been aware of the fundamental moral orientation of American realism. Joel Chandler Harris immediately recognized
that "there is not in our fictive literature a more wholesome
book than 'Huckleberry Finn.'. . . We are taught [by it] the
lesson of honesty, justice, and mercy." Unlike many contemporary critics, Harris realized that the ethical force of
Huckleberry Finn and the other realistic novels was not
based upon external spiritual forces but upon the confronta-
tion of human beings in a humanly created social environment. The realists' morality is intrinsic, integral, relativistic;
it arises from the characters and the narrative action, rather
than being superimposed upon them. Significant fiction has
always been ethical, and the realists come to rather conventional conclusions about the qualities men must have in
dealing with each other—honesty, justice, mercy, love. What
is new in 1885 is that these qualities are no longer sought in
an external, transcendental system of values. Realistic protagonists are forced to work out their own codes of behavior,
appropriate to their individual circumstances.

Howells, James, and Mark Twain do not professedly teach
or preach. They do not step to the front of the stage and tell the
reader how to interpret their puppets. On the other hand, the
realists do not ignore interpretation. Since the moral arises
from the fabric of the fictional experience, interpretation is
built into the narrative. The reader makes the interpretation
for himself, but if he is a careful reader he makes the interpretation that the author desires. The reader's freedom to
choose, like the realist's "objectivity," is largely an illusion.

[Critic] Alfred Kazin has remarked that Howells' morality,

like Tolstoy's, meant "the relation of man to his society." The observation is valid for all the realists, and the fiction of the mid-1880s explores the relations between man and society in a variety of ways. *Adventures of Huckleberry Finn* contains a double pattern: the condemnation of religious, political, and social opinions which are held by fools and exploited by knaves and the affirmation of brotherhood through the relation of Huck and Jim. Huck faces a dilemma common in realistic fiction. When he finds that Jim has been sold back into slavery by the King, Huck is forced to decide between a fixed code of public morality and an inner ethical impulse—a conflict which he resolves at the climax of *Huckleberry Finn:*

> I was a trembling, because I'd got to decide, forever, betwixt two things, and I knowed it. I studied a minute, sort of holding my breath, and then says to myself:
>
> "All right, then, I'll go to hell."

Huck chooses hell and humanity; his sound heart triumphs over the conscience which has been deformed by a morally corrupt society. . . .

Like Huck Finn, Silas Lapham struggles with a difficult and lonely moral decision for which he has no precedent, and, like Huck, he wins a moral victory. Lapham's final rise is an ethical one, climaxed when he refuses to sell his western milling property, which he knows to be of little value, to English buyers. This decision is made difficult by Lapham's cascading series of financial disasters and more difficult by the apparent dishonesty of the Englishmen, who represent "rich and charitable" investors who will not feel the loss of the money which could save Lapham. A further loophole is provided by Colonel Lapham's ex-partner Rogers, who offers to serve as a middleman in the purchase and thus relieve Lapham of any legal responsibility. He is tempted and confused, but Lapham resists the offer until it is no longer feasible. Morally strengthened by this victory of hesitation, he is then easily able to refuse to sell the paint works in Vermont to a New York agent who is unaware of the declining market value of Lapham's mineral paint. Silas Lapham's fall from business, from wealth, and from Beacon Street is complete. He retires to his Vermont farm, and taking his poverty with better grace than his success, closes his story with a laconic but sincere testimony to morality: "I don't know as I should always say it paid; but if I done it, and the thing was to do over again, right in the same way, I guess I should have to do it.". . .

In the closing pages of *Silas Lapham,* Mr. Sewell (one of several peripatetic characters who appear in different Howells novels) observes that "we can trace the operation of evil in the physical world . . . but I'm more and more puzzled about it in the moral world. There its course is often so very obscure. . . ." Henry James would thoroughly agree, for, characteristically, the morality of his novels is less obvious than that of Howells, but no less central to his artistic purpose. *The Bostonians* is a novel without a hero, and emphatically a novel without a heroine. There is no moral mouthpiece, no center of reference, for Basil Ransom is no more "right" than the Bostonians to whom he is a foil. The moral, as usual for James, must be drawn by inference, by implication—ultimately, by character. With the exception of Verena Tarrant, the malleable prize, all of the characters, whether reformers or reactionaries, Northerners or Southerners, are motivated by selfishness. The main conflict, that of Basil and Olive over Verena, is one of will rather than of love, and each wants her for his own satisfaction. Selah Tarrant, like Hollingsworth, his spiritual ancestor in Hawthorne's *Blithedale Romance,* is a "moralist without moral sense," who rents his daughter to Olive on a yearly basis. The reform movement itself, with its sacrifices and its martyrdoms, is seen as an exercise in ego. The entire group is transfixed on the shrill point of Olive's despairing concern for herself: "I shall see nothing but shame and ruin!" The novel's coda is provided, ironically, by self-seeking Mrs. Tarrant: "It's the most horrible, wicked, immoral selfishness I ever heard in my life!". . .

Howells, James, and Mark Twain agree that we fully become human beings only when we escape the prison of the ego. This affirmation of basic human values should exculpate the realists from charges of immorality and amorality, although such moral themes are not new, by any means. Huck's raft was preceded by a good many vessels, the *Pequod* among them, for the lesson of the monkey-rope is as applicable to Huck and Jim as it is to Ishmael and Queequeg, even though Twain, characteristically, refuses to editorialize or overtly symbolize the relationship. What the realists contribute in their discussion of human values is the emphasis on the complexity of moral choice and the necessity of individual decision in a human context, unassisted by external spiritual forces. And these values are dramatized rather than sermonized in the novels of the mid-1880s . . . for [, as Howells wrote,] the realist refuses to "stand about in his scene, talking it over with his hands in his pockets, interrupting the action, and spoiling the illusion."

Realism Rejected Sentimental Culture

Everett Carter

Everett Carter identifies a fundamental conflict between the Realist and Sentimental views of the world
in late nineteenth century American culture. He
maintains that one way in which Realism defined itself was through its opposition to Sentimental American literature. Sentimentalism dominated American
culture for much of the nineteenth century, and its
fiction followed a certain formula that attracted
droves of readers. A typical sentimental novel might
include stock character types such as a beautiful, virtuous heroine, and a chivalrous, handsome gentlemen who inevitably wins her hand in marriage. It
might complicate the plot with a scheming villain or
a cruel parent who seeks to thwart the progress of
their love. Bombastic language, tearful scenes, and
overwrought emotions usually accompanied sentimental fiction's predictable plots. Sentimental culture lives on today in the form of soap operas and
mass market romances, and fulfills the same needs
in readers now as it did then. According to Carter,
William Dean Howells, Mark Twain and other Realists believed Sentimentalism created a false and
damaging view of life, and they sought to expose its
falsehoods in both their fiction and their critical essays. Everett Carter was a Professor at the University
of California at Davis. He wrote *Howells and the Age
of Realism* (1954) and *The American Idea: The Literary Response to American Optimism* (1977).

By 1866, . . . back from his European withdrawal, and hired,
at the suggestion of James Russell Lowell, as assistant editor
of the *Atlantic*, William Dean Howells, creature of his times,

worshipper of the actual, but with a strain of idealism and mysticism which could never be erased, one-time dabbler in sentimental poetry and fiction, had resolutely set himself against his previous tendencies and the prevailing current of his times. His initial impulse to begin to form a credo of criticism and then of creation—a yard stick by which to judge the works of others and then his own work—was a negative impulse; he simply was against the kind of prettified falsehoods which were passing as current in American literature during the 1860's and '70's. . . .

The next thirty years witnessed the growth of a group of American writers bound together by their disdain for the meretricious and their allegiance to the real, as they saw it. Some of them wrote well, many of them wrote poorly; the value of what they finally did had no necessary relation to their motives. Often Twain and occasionally Howells were able to achieve the justness of internal relations which makes for artistic distinction. Eggleston, Tourgée, Bret Harte almost invariably failed, almost always slipped into one kind of sentimentalism while they were attacking another. But they all partook of a common impulse—a desire to satirize false views of life, and the literature which encouraged them. By finding in anti-sentiment a motive for creation, these writers were underscoring the parallel between their age and other ages of reason in Western culture. . . .

THE REJECTION OF SENTIMENTAL VIEWS OF EUROPE

Howells' first considerable works were two travel sketches of Italy, the first entitled *Venetian Life*, the second *Italian Journeys*. Howells showed a close observation of, and sympathetic interest in, the small, homely details of Italian existence. His cook, her family, the gondoliers, a policeman, a cripple trying on a suit of clothes in a local store—these are the things of which his two travel books were made. . . .

Involved in this discovery of . . . Howells that people, even in the heretofore culturally idolized and feared Old World, were essentially one in their common humanity, was an intellectual patriotism, an assertion of the equality of America, and hence the dignity and value of American civilization. This kind of cultural patriotism endowed the early anti-sentimentalism of Howells, as it did the attacks upon falsity by . . . Twain, with a basic appeal to his American audience. *Venetian Life* sold well and was well reviewed. In all three major periodical reviews, the word "delightful" appeared; readers remarked upon its "pleasant flavor of individuality" and its "beauty of finish"; there was surprised admiration for the native gentility of someone born in Ohio, and for the implicit attack upon sentimentality in the work. "Most tourists," one reviewer emphasized, "go to Venice with *Childe Harold* and Rogers' *Italy* in their minds and hands."[1] But to Howells, "Lord Byron is neither a hero nor a historian . . . and he quietly tells the truth about the Bridge of Sighs.". . .

And then a year after his own success, a volume came across Howells' reviewing desk which climaxed this series of travel books written by pioneer realists to tell the truth about the parent culture of Europe. It was called *The Innocents Abroad* and reminded Howells that there was a writer appearing on the American scene who, like himself, was dedicating his life to the truthful reporting of that which he saw, and to the blasting of sentimental falsehoods. . . .

MARK TWAIN'S REJECTION OF THE OLD WORLD

His purpose, Twain declared at the very outset of his book of travels, was the purpose of . . . Howells: to "suggest to the reader how *he* would be likely to see Europe and the East if he looked at them with his own eyes instead of the eyes of those who traveled . . . before him." At once, then, he identified himself with the American reader; he would make "small pretense of showing anyone how he *ought* to look at objects." He would let them look through his eyes. He was an innocent, with other innocents, and he reported what he saw, with the directness of the child. When he found something he could genuinely admire, he told about it; but when he found pretense and humbug, when he saw something distorted by sentimentalism, he stripped the veil from it by comparing romantic exterior with inner truth: for example, his description of the Portuguese boatmen "with brass rings in their ears, and fraud in their hearts." He could appreciate the Europeans' ability to forget the work of the day when it was done; he was pleased to find his party of tourists relax their pace; he noticed "the absence of hog wallows, broken fences, cow-lots, unpainted houses" and the presence of "cleanliness, grace, taste in adorning and beautifying." But

1. *Childe Harold* was one of Romantic poet George Lord Byron's most famous works. Rogers' *Italy* was a popular middle and late nineteenth century guidebook.

the ignorance, the superstition, the fraud which masquer-
ades as quaintness, the squalor that pretends to beauty—
these he demolished with mining-camp humor. Of the
Azores he saw that there was "not a modern plow in the islands, or a threshing-machine," for at any attempt to introduce them the good Portuguese "crossed himself and prayed
God to shield him from all blasphemous desire to know
more than his father did before him." In Italy he found "the
home of priestcraft—the land of poverty, indolence, and
everlasting unaspiring worthlessness." In Venice, he felt it "a
sort of sacrilege to disturb the glamour of old romance" that
pictured her as a thing of beauty, but he was compelled to
report that in place of the "fairy boat" and the "gay gondolier
in silken doublet" there was actually "an inky, rusty old ca-
noe" and a "mangy, barefooted guttersnipe."

Where other travellers had come to worship at the shrine
of European culture, Twain was an unabashed practical
Yankee, who liked to revel in the dryest details. . . . In front
of the Last Supper, he looked hard, looked again, and could
only report that the colors were "dimmed with age"; the
countenances "scaled and marred," and nearly all expression "gone from them." Then he saw others about him,
standing entranced before it and ejaculating over the
"matchless coloring" where there was no color, the delicacy
and feeling where there was only a dead blur, and he could
only turn away with wryly good-natured sadness at the ability of some to see that which was not there.

He never gave up pricking the bubble of pretentious un-
truths about the glories of our parent culture, and about the
supposed superiority of its storied, aristocratic past to the
democratic bourgeois American present. His two best works
of historical fiction, *The Prince and the Pauper* and *A Connecticut Yankee in King Arthur's Court*, are excursions into
the past not for nostalgia or escape, but for demonstration of
the superiority of republicanism to aristocracy, industrialism to agrarianism, and reason to superstition. . . .

HOWELL'S ATTACK ON SENTIMENTALISM'S MYTHS

As Howells did in his trans-Atlantic sketches, so he did in his
writings on the American scene. When, after taking up the
assistant editorship of the *Atlantic* in 1866, he turned his eyes
upon the humanity of his own country, he began the same
comic attack upon the lie that gave his books of foreign travel

TWAIN, THE SOUTH, AND SIR WALTER SCOTT

*Mark Twain often attacked the influence Sentimental cul-
ture and the Romance had in the South. To his mind, they
encouraged a misguided and damaging view of life. In this
passage, taken from* Life on the Mississippi *(1883), he laments
the continuing influence of Scottish novelist and poet Sir Walter
Scott, who wrote a number of successful historical romances of
which* Rob Roy *is the most famous.*

Sir Walter Scott is probably responsible for the Capitol building;
for it is not conceivable that this little sham castle would ever
have been built if he had not run the people mad, a couple of
generations ago, with his mediæval romances. The South has
not yet recovered from the debilitating influence of his books.
Admiration of his fantastic heroes and their grotesque
"chivalry" doings and romantic juvenilities still survives here,
in an atmosphere in which is already perceptible the whole
some and practical nineteenth-century smell of cotton-factories
and locomotives; and traces of its inflated language and other
windy humbuggeries survive along with it. It is pathetic
enough, that a whitewashed castle, with turrets and things—
materials all ungenuine within and without, pretending to be
what they are not—should ever have been built in this otherwise honorable place; but it is much more pathetic to see this
architectural falsehood undergoing restoration and perpetua-
tion in our day, when it would have been so easy to let dyna-
mite finish what a charitable fire began, and then devote this
restoration-money to the building of something genuine.

Reprinted from Mark Twain, *Life on the Mississippi* (New York: Penguin, 1984),
285–286.

their secure place in the history of the anti-sentimental. In
both his criticism and his first hesitant steps in fiction he
showed that his underlying motive was to oppose the flood
of literature which was not teaching men the truth, but was
telling them the kinds of sugar-coated lies which would satisfy their preconceptions. . . .

From 1881 to 1885, Howells devoted himself to the writing of fiction, with only the occasional break of an article
like that on Henry James, Jr., which set the English critics on
their ears by declaring that James' art of fiction was a finer
one than that of Dickens and Thackeray. But in 1885, he returned to regular reviewing for *Harper's Monthly* and for six
years he wrote a monthly feature, "The Editor's Study," in

which he fought the battle for realism and against sentimentalism. During these years sentimental fiction had assumed a new guise—the historical romance; and it was with
the sentimental version of the historical romance that Howells crossed swords in what became one of the bitterest literary battles in American critical history.

We must repeat our words of caution here about the nature of these difficult terms "romance" and "romantic." "Romance" as a way of looking at life through literature which,
like a poem, is at once "more elevated and more mechanical
than a novel"; romance in which "you concede the premises
as in a poem, and after that you hold the author only to a po-
etical consistency"—to this way of seeking truth through literature Howells was, we have already seen, friendly and understanding. He had some reservations about the ability of a
writer of less than superior talents to handle the recreation of
the past: "it is hard to get nature to take part in one's little effects when it is an affair of contemporary life; if it is an affair
of life in the past her co-operation is still more reluctant." But
the great writer, he felt, could understand the oneness of all
people at all times, and make his work as true when it concerned remote times and places as when it concerned the
now and the here. . . .

But when lesser talents tried the historical romance, the result was simply another example of lying about life which
Howells knew was bad art and worse morality. He tried several times to find another term for "bad" historical fiction. Fiction, he once said, can be used to portray either the ideal or the
real; "that which it is loath to serve is the unreal"; for the "unreal," he suggested, "we have no name for but romanticistic."

Since others, however, called sentimental historical fiction "romance," Howells usually went along with them; and
it is true, of course, that the writers of historical tales usually
deal with painted dolls going through stereotyped patterns
of action in front of papier-mâché settings. And towards this
kind of fiction, Howells' attitude varied between scornful
condescension and positive distaste. Sometimes he would
say that this kind of writing might serve a harmless, although useless service for readers who cannot face life but
must see it through the mists of distance "in which all the
disagreeable details shall be lost.". . . But more often he was
bitter about this use of his craft to enable people to escape
from the realities of the life about them, for he saw that only

through facing these realities could they cure some of the diseases that were corrupting the American life he loved. . . .

The false and mistaken sentimentalist view of life was the major target not only of Howells' criticism, but of his fiction. Beginning with his first sketches in 1870 and 1871, and continuing through his last novel which appeared in 1920, he consistently made his opposition to the sentimental view of life an important motive of his work. . . .

TWAIN'S ATTACK ON JAMES FENIMORE COOPER

The well-aimed bullet of ridicule was easily the most effective weapon used against sentimentalism. . . . Twain's most detailed work of literary criticism, as a matter of fact, came from his compulsion to detail "Fenimore Cooper's Literary Offenses" after two professors and an English novelist had combined to declare Cooper a great artist in fiction. . . . "Cooper's art has some defects," he asserted with the air of calculated seriousness which often prefaced his wild flings of satiric exaggeration. And then he began his attack: "In one place in the *Deerslayer*, and in the restricted space of two-thirds of a page, Cooper has scored 114 offenses against literary art out of a possible 115. It breaks the record." The rules governing literary art, Twain made it clear, should be the rules of the realist: that literary art should have a "life-likeness" and "seeming reality"; that it should deal with the life the author knows, and deal with it accurately; not that the author must try to reproduce life, or confine himself purely to the level of objective experience; far from it; after all, this was the author of the *Connecticut Yankee* talking. But literary artists should "confine themselves to possibilities and let miracles alone; or, if they venture a miracle, the author must so plausibly set it forth as to make it look possible and reasonable."

Cooper fell hopelessly short of these standards, Mark insisted. Against the measure of the rule that "the personages in a tale shall be alive, except in the case of corpses, and that the reader shall be able to tell the corpses from the others," Cooper's all-pure heroines and all-heroic heroes, his noble savages and intrepid frontiersmen, dwindled into false nothingness. Against the laws which demand at least a kind of internal consistency, Cooper also sinned. It is expected, said Mark, that "when a personage talks like an illustrated, gilt-edged, tree-calf, hand-tooled, seven dollar Friendship's Offering in the beginning of a paragraph, he shall not talk like a negro minstrel in the end of it. But this rule is flung down and danced upon in the *Deerslayer* tale."

Above all, Cooper had no real knowledge of what he was writing about: "one of his acute Indian experts, Chingach-gook," pronounced "Chicago," turned a running stream out of its course and found the tracks of the last person in the slush of its bed. "No," said Twain sadly, "even the eternal laws of Nature have to vacate when Cooper wants to put up a delicate job of woodcraft on the reader." And he summarized his diatribe by declaring that Cooper "saw nearly all things as through a glass eye, darkly."

TWAIN'S SATIRE OF SENTIMENTALISM AND GREED

This ridicule of Cooper came at the end of the nineteenth century, but Twain's scorn for the glass eye of the literary falsifier had been evident as early as *The Innocents Abroad* and had been a consistent theme in his work. . . . As he wrote to Mrs. Mary Mason Fairbanks, one of the "innocents" with whom he was abroad in 1867, he had but one desire: to be "authentic." With this as his standard, he could never pass up an occasion to attack those who were telling falsehoods about the life he knew and loved. When he and Charles Dudley Warner wrote the most elaborate work of satiric realism written by Americans in the nineteenth century—the joint effort they called *The Gilded Age,* thereby giving a name to an entire era—they wrote an attack in fiction upon sentimentalism in literature as it operated in the social and economic and political life of America.

Two stories were written by the collaborators, and it has been conventional to say that the book falls apart because the two appear to have only a remote connection. But viewed as an attack on a false view of reality, the two stories are seen immediately to have an organic connection. One story they told was an imaginative account of Mark's own history and the history of his family, and a projection into the future of what could have happened to them, given the kind of people they were. For the fictional Hawkins family, like the real Clemens clan, had been victimized by the great sentimental myth of financial success, the myth which assured Americans that fabulous wealth was always available for those energetic enough to get it. As a counterpoint to the story of the downfall of the Hawkins family, Twain and

Warner wrote of the Bolton family and Philip Sterling; the Boltons found that speculation could bring only misery, but they were rescued by the hard work of Philip, who turned from will-o'-the-wisp adventuring after gold mines to prospecting for good, black, productive, unromantic coal. The interplay of the two stories made the moral clear: dreams of glory bring disaster; only hard work brings happiness. The Hawkins family was a family cursed by a sentimental dream, a dream without reasonable foundation in the world of reality, a dream of great wealth to come from the 75,000 acres of Tennessee land in which Silas Hawkins had speculated. The dream, Washington Hawkins realized at the end, was an illusion which he chased "as children chase butterflies." He lifted the curse of the dream by tearing up the tax bill for the land, and letting it go, and with it, the false hopes of speedy and painless riches.

Realism Reflects a Common Vision of Everyday Life

Edwin H. Cady

Any attempt to define Realism runs into problems. For instance, how does one define what is "real," and how can fiction make a claim to represent "reality"? Edwin H. Cady firstly examines the revolt on the part of the American Realists against the excesses of Romanticism. He then emphasizes the extent to which the Realists placed complex characters, forced to make complex moral decisions, at the forefront of their novels. This selection ends with Cady's attempt to create a working definition of what exactly Realism in late nineteenth and early twentieth century American literature was. The principle behind Cady's definition is that of "common vision." By this, Cady means that society is characterized by commonly shared experiences and beliefs. It is into this social and cultural framework that we incorporate the uniqueness of our own relationship with the objects and events of the world in which we live. Much as we accept the necessity of certain rules governing a particular game we might play, we accept the notion of an underlying "reality" in the world. As a literary form, Realism can be defined by the extent to which, through a detailed analysis of society and culture, it highlights the extent and importance of commonly shared, "everyday" experiences. Aside from his work on American Realism, Edwin H. Cady taught English at Duke University, and he wrote the definitive biography of William Dean Howells.

The concern common to the . . . principal American realists is concern for vision. They point toward a literature which

Excerpted from *The Light of Common Day: Realism in American Fiction*, by Edwin H. Cady (Bloomington, IN: Indiana University Press, 1971). Reprinted with permission from the author.

rests upon a particular theory of vision. In a preliminary way, I should define it as: *Realism,* a theory of Common Vision. Though it would take a very long time to elaborate the helpful qualifications of that stark phrase, at this point I should like to emphasize the useful ambiguity of "common." It may mean "common" as average, ordinary, normal, democratic. It may also mean "common" as shared, general, normative, perhaps even universal.

The aim here is to make a beginning toward lending content to "realism" and "realistic." The hope is to enrich the vocabulary of literary discussion by adding precision to key terms. By examining a historical moment of self-proclaimed realism, perhaps we can move from the verifiable ideas and attitudes of "a realism" toward more abstract and generally applicable meanings. The realism I know best is that of American literature of roughly 1860–1910, and I shall therefore take my examples from it. . . .

We have become accustomed in the past two centuries to the general pattern of a literary revolt. First comes ennui with the worn conventions of overpopular fashions. Yearning for newness leads to youthful cries of back to nature, and Young Turks riot in the pages of little magazines. Something like that happened with the brilliant generation of Americans who became more or less thirty years old in 1870. They were fed up with romanticism. They expended magnificent resources of wit and creative energy to burlesque it out of public countenance. They defined their dearest wishes for expression and artistic success in contradiction to it. They welcomed eagerly a newness which promised to set them free.

To say it briefly, intellectual newness came to this generation in that form of nineteenth-century scientism ordinarily associated with . . . [scientist Charles] Darwin. For this middle generation of American Darwinists, exposed in youth to the old idealism, Thomas Huxley's[1] agnosticism seemed the properest response to the newness. It led them toward a vaguely positivistic factualism.[2] And, insofar as they were writers, it reinforced their ennui to create a burningly reductive antiromanticism. . . . Henry James may, as he perceived to his chagrin, have "cut the cable" in *The American* and let the balloon of experience float away into the ro-

1. a famous defender of Darwin's theories   2. a philosophy that maintains people cannot know anything beyond what is perceived through the five senses

mantic "disconnected and uncontrolled." But in *The Portrait of a Lady* he was soon engaged in the realist's joyous game of shooting down romantic balloons, piercing them through to let the gassy hot air out and drop them back to earth. A like effect was the aim of Mark Twain's unending campaign against "Sir Walter Scottism." Young William Lyon Phelps, interviewing Howells, reported that he never saw a man laugh so consumedly as Howells while numbering the follies of romance. Howells once described the zest of critical warfare as the fun of "banging the Babes of romance about."

THE DISTINCTION BETWEEN ROMANTICISM, REALISM, AND NATURALISM

The serious side of their antiromantic attitude showed in what became the humanism of these realists. One can distinguish the realist from the romanticist on the one side and the naturalist on the other by precisely this distinction. The romantic, in the long run, is concerned with the ideal, the transcendent, the superhuman. The naturalist is concerned with vast forces, heredity and environment, a world of brute chance, with what we share of animality, with ultimate reduction, the subhuman. As against the romantic, the realist was certainly reductive. There is type significance in the fact that the fathers of Howells and James were Swedenborgians.[3] Both sons had been taught to believe in a double vision according to the doctrine of "correspondence": above every physical existence there hovered spiritual significance, an angel, an essence, an eternal destiny. As agnostics, both in time felt compelled to blot transcendence out from the realm of intellectual fact. Their vision fell from an upward to a level plane where it focused upon man and his life in the world.

THE IMPORTANCE OF CHARACTER IN REALISM

Such humanism produced important technical, that is literary, as well as metaphysical and ethical effects. It led realists to deemphasize plot: for them character, the simple, separate person, came to count; not flashing action or terrific fable. By the same token, literary emotional and sentimental heights, what Howells was to call "effectism," were cut

---

3. followers of theologian Emanuel Swedenborg, who believed there is a causal relationship between the spiritual and natural worlds

down. Obviously it would seem false to make believe that nonsublime people should pretend to superhuman emotions. In realistic hands, the tools of the novelist would be devoted to the main end of bodying forth characters in their habits as they lived. As a corollary there came a shift in their method to what might be called the imploding symbol, to symbols which functioned to intensify inwardly the total effect of a novel, which did not refer outside the novel to general meaning. A second corollary became an emphasis upon contemporaneousness. The historical novel came to be thought a psychological anomaly.

THE REALIST METHOD

As is already apparent, no serious writer could have rested in mere negations. Burlesquing romance went well in a humor-mad age. But serious literature required a "positive realism," methods developed to express and present the new vision of the common man in his world. The realists' favorite positive technique became what they called the "dramatic method." It demanded the suppression of the "author" from his scene in the novel as the playwright was excluded from all drama except that of "romantic irony" with its deliberately suicidal destruction of illusion. It demanded the creation of "transparent" narrators who seemed never to intrude between the reader and his vision of the characters, who spoke, when "scenes" and "pictures" could not simply be presented, in an unobtrusively "middle" voice. It regarded plot as the account of a breaking in upon and subsequent retreat from an instant of that seamless continuity which is life and so, once more, suppressed plot as much as editors and public would permit. . . .

REALISM AS THE LITERATURE OF DEMOCRACY

With their scorn for the romantically unique, intense, or superhuman, and with their humanistic concern for persons, the American realists sympathized with democracy. Realism as democracy became a significant feature of the literary movement. Increasingly, the writers concentrated on the commonness of the lives of common men. They thought the common significant because it was fresh to literature (that is, never really done before), because it was intrinsically real, and because it was uniquely important from the "universal" side of the implication of "common." They were led in turn to reinterpret the American Dream and use the language of Emerson and of Whitman without transcendental reference. The realists dreamed not of "the American Adam" but the superiority of the vulgar. When Matthew Arnold foresaw the ultimate damnation of democracy in the absence of distinction from America, Howells rejoiced. If a nation, he remarked, could produce Emerson and Hawthorne, Lincoln, Grant, and Mark Twain and still escape distinction, there was true hope for it. Precisely the same attitudes Twain immortalized in certain adventures of Huck Finn and of Hank Morgan, the Connecticut Yankee. And, after his fashion, Henry James expressed cognate perceptions in portraits of that most contemptible of men, the Europeanized American.

REALISM AND TRAVEL

The evolution of the travel book and of the perceptions of cultural relativity which the practice of travel writing engendered in the writers helped give rise to realism, and thereafter a natural concern of the realist was the international theme. Henry James on the Europeanized American, Howells's exploration of the "conventional-unconventional" conflict, and Twain's transmutation of the frontier humorist's war against the Eastern snob all came to the same point. Of necessity, the realist fought snobbery and factitious aristocracy. In doing so he rang every imaginable change upon the theme of the Innocent Abroad. We are far from having exhausted the meaning inherent in the famous opposed curves of the attitudes of James and Twain toward American values, early Twain against early James and late against late. And Howells, sharing with and often anticipating both, arrived at his [Utopian] visions of Tolstoi and Altruria in a fascinating kind of mediation between them.

REALISM'S MORAL VISION

A fourth characteristic of this American realism was its moral vision. As one may see in the familiar writings of Howells and James—*The Rise of Silas Lapham,* "The Beast in the Jungle"—essential to their moral vision was an active disbelief in the health or safety of romantic individualism. The same sense gives resonance to Huck Finn's famous decision to go to hell for Nigger Jim. Conformity to the code of Tom Sawyer's misshapen "civilization" would have brought Huck the sensations of "salvation" for his "ornery" soul and the comfort of self-respect for his "low-down" and outcast character. He had almost chosen respectable self-identity and the sanction to stand upright in an individualistic culture. Instead, he chose damnation: that is, solidarity (as [novelist] Edward Bellamy would call his religion beyond egotism) or "complicity," as Howells repeatedly termed it, with Jim—in hell, if necessary. A like self-sacrifice accords Jim his climactic meed of heroism when he steps out of hiding, presumably into bondage again if not death by torture, when the frantic doctor calls for aid to wounded Tom Sawyer.

These were the attitudes, consciously antiromantic, which led Stephen Crane to conclude that, "The final wall of the wise man's thought . . . is Human Kindness of course." Their reduction . . . of morality from sublimity to solidarity made the common vision appear essential to a right grasp of life. Therefore Howells announced that a bad novel was a school of crime. And [critic] Hjalmar Hjorth Boyesen, with Scandinavian solemnity, backed him up by arguing that "romance" deprives its devotees of "sound standards of judgement," whereas realism reveals "the significance of common facts and events . . . the forces that govern the world . . . and the logic of life."

Their moral vision reinforced the realists' affinities for democracy and contemporaneousness and brought them toward effective insights into the human problems of the historically unique industrial culture forming around them. Those insights stimulated their alliances with the growing sentiment of reform. The preservation and extension of democracy, Populism, Progressivism, Nationalism (Bellamy's, that is), unions and the labor movement, socialism, anti-imperialism, and, perhaps most permanently, a long-continuing critical examination of the American Business Mind, occupied in various ways much of the thought and creative inquiry of the American realists as their movement matured. . . .

REALISM AND PSYCHOLOGY

Finally, since some sort of change seems to be historically inevitable, it was proper that American realism should develop in such a way as to prepare for its own succession. The writers moved toward an increasingly psychological realism, propelled by two major forces. One of these was the displacement of positivism from its dominance of late nineteenth-century thought. A decade like the nineties, which began with William

James's *Psychology* and ended with the unleashing of those electronic factors in physical thought which produced Henry Adams's image of "himself lying in the Gallery of Machines at the Great Exposition of 1900, his historical neck broken by the sudden irruption of forces totally new," was bound to loosen the grip of positivism on the imagination. A second force, however, arose from the practices of realistic fiction itself. The more one confronted the mystery of persons living out their fates and struggling toward death, the more his scrutiny turned from the outward sign to the inward process. Howells noticed in 1903, when he was writing a novel Freudian in everything but specifically Viennese terminology, that all the realists had been turning to psychology. Indeed, many had been flirting with psychic phenomena as far-flung as the claims of spiritualism. . . .

Obviously, however, the methods and angles of vision of realism could not be finally satisfactory for the exploration of psychology. The more one moved from the seen toward the unseeable, from the common toward the private vision, the more other methods appealed. The movement toward symbolism of the late James was as natural as the movement into stream of consciousness for [Irish modernist James] Joyce. Thus realism prepared the way for its succession.

THE PROBLEM OF DEFINING REALISM

One must, it goes without saying, be aware that the Americans did not work in isolation. They participated in a huge, though ill-defined, international realistic school. . . . Obviously such names as those of Flaubert, Zola, and Daudet in France; Turgenev, Tolstoi, Dostoevski, Gogol in Russia; Galdós, Palacio Valdés, and Pardo-Bazan in Spain; Björnson, Ibsen, and Brandes in Scandinavia; Hauptmann in Germany, Verga in Italy, Hardy and then Bennett and Galsworthy in England, stand out. I could not pretend to discuss the grand pattern. But perhaps I can propose certain general considerations, more or less abstracted from the American experience, for clarifying the terms "realism" and "realistic."

As a beginning, I wish to propose two distinctions which I should like to make precise. The first is to distinguish between "realism" as a literary mode and "reality" in every extraliterary sense. The second is to distinguish the literary situation in which apparently realistic means have been employed to secure final, total effects which are not realistic from the work which does finally, in totality, achieve realism. Ultimately, I shall propose a general definition of realism which might survive these distinctions.

Most ordinary, dictionary definitions of realism are circular. Realism, they say, deals with what is real (if not merely with what is unpleasant). The [Oxford English Dictionary] . . . is a notorious offender in this respect, and the Webster International says: "In art and literature, fidelity to nature or to real life." Apart from bald circularity, there are several objections to such definitions. They provide no means of distinguishing realistic from other literature. We do not have, and are not likely soon to achieve, general agreement about the nature of reality—the qualities of "nature" and "real life." Furthermore, such questions are metaphysical and philosophical, and we are after a literary definition. We need to discard the notion that realism must rest upon a discarded nineteenth-century and vaguely positivistic factualism—or, indeed, rest upon any philosophical realism—and look further.

Questions of definition in literary studies are customarily (and I think rightly) referred to the effects of literature upon the reader. Consideration of such an essentially psychological question sometimes leads to a definition in which literature is called "realistic" because it is so vivid, powerful, profound, or exact in its effect upon the receiving imagination that it "seems real." But this definition, I think, confuses "realism" with literary success. The essence of literary art is to "seem real" in the sense of captivating the reader's imagination, no matter what the qualities of the experience to which imagination is led in the chains of art. That way, all true literature becomes "realistic." But whatever means everything means nothing. "Realism" as a term is destroyed. If it is to have any viable critical use, the term must distinguish some kind of true, of successful, literature from other kinds. The same dead end is reached by the argument that "realism" should be taken to mean "faithful to the writer's unique and personal sense of reality." Every sound expressive success, regardless of variances among authors' faiths and visions, would become "realistic.". . .

REALISM AS OPPOSED TO VERISIMILITUDE

Let us turn on to a perhaps useful distinction between "realism" and "verisimilitude." It is my impression that much confusion in the discussion of realism has been caused by failure to attend to the difference between the effect of one part of a work of literature and the effect of the whole. Because, for instance, there are moments of strategic attention to homely detail in *The Faerie Queene* and in *Henry IV,* Part I, it is sometimes said that they are realistic. They are in total effect heroic, chivalric, exotic, rather romantic, and, in the case of *The Faerie Queene,* allegorical-fantastic: great works, but not realism.

The same point might be made by examining such very different pieces as the opening pages of *Gulliver's Travels* and Poe's famous tale "The Descent into the Maelstrom." In Swift's opening there is a wonderfully "voiced" and detailed account of the ordinary career of a wilful lad who became a commonplace ship's surgeon. We are led comfortably into an apparently normal memoir of travel and adventure by sea, suspicion at rest, disbelief suspended. And all at once we find ourselves in Lilliput. The tactic is obvious. In Poe's tale we are drawn with the narrator into a scene of horror, hanging with his ship on the wall of a mammoth whirlpool down the sides of which we may slip inexorably to destruction as gravity slowly overcomes centrifugal force. Both the unity and Gothic effect of the tale demand, however, that the narrator shall escape while we, at least through the duration of the tale, shall believe in his escape. How to do this? Poe resorts to a brilliantly precise description of just how it was that objects whirled and swam, sank or stayed up in the maelstrom. We see with the narrator that he *must* lash himself to a barrel and leap into the torrential wall of water, abandoning his fear-paralyzed brother to destruction with the heavy ship. The total effect is one of fantastic horror and release, Gothicism at its best.

If one were to take the moments of what might look like realism in all four works to authorize calling the works realistic, he would have lost, at least to that extent, the grounds for differentiating among them. Yet it is clearly important critically to avoid confounding *The Faerie Queene, Henry IV,* Part I, *Gulliver's Travels,* and "The Descent into the Maelstrom." To call them all realistic would be to obscure the essential literary qualities of each; for each has as the essential qualities of its greatness, qualities not realistic. Hence the usefulness of distinguishing local, partial, even fragmentary uses of realistic effects to contribute to what will in the long run and total effect be nonrealistic, from what achieves realism in final effect. The partial or local effects I would call "verisimilitude," reserving the word "realism" for the other.

REALISM'S "COMMON VISION"

What, then, to come finally to the point, should be called "realism"? . . . By way of attempting an answer, I wish to recur to the earliest pages of this discussion and suggest that literary realism be seen as dependent upon a theory of common vision. That theory rests upon the combination of a theory of literary art with an amateur theory of perception.

First, the theory of common vision assumes that art-technical (the words of the text on the page in their patterns) arouses in the reader art as experience by impelling his imagination to create that experience subjectively. It observes that there is some, presently obscure, relationship between the experience a reader gets (or can make) from "non-art," what we call "life," and the experience he derives from art. . . . For instance, one sees a view, sees a painting, reads a poetic description: and "feels" landscape. One "sees" a ghost, he sees *Hamlet,* he reads *Hamlet.* One eats at a cafeteria, he reads of so eating. It is not to be doubted that art as technique will strategically have shaped art-experience. We can apparently not quite know how that non-art experience occurs which may range from foggy undifferentiatedness to something explosive or fateful. The point to be clung to is that there persistently are varietal likenesses between instances of the two orders of experience. That is why one should be loath to deny relationship between literature and "reality" even while observing all the caveats noted earlier.

It might therefore be possible to propose a positive and general definition of realism as representing the art-variety of a "real" order of non-art experience—an order, that is, which even those who held to deeply opposed temperamental and metaphysical notions of ultimate reality might agree to accept as "real" in some useful and common, even though minimal, sense. That variety I should propose to be the socially agreed upon "common vision" which permits ordinary processes of law and social control to succeed, creates the possibility of games, makes most technical, economic, and even educational enterprises possible. That world of the common vision is, indeed, what is ordinarily referred to as "reality." But, of course, it has not been reality for many people of the past as it is not for many—and especially for many artists—today. . . .

The world of common vision does certainly not in itself encompass all the varieties of "reality" available to art experience. But it certainly is, on the other hand, in fact one sort of reality common to almost everybody. It provides the ground for one kind, a dominant variety, of non-art experience. There must surely be a variety of art-experience cognate to the world of common vision. Regardless, then, of whether it is absolutely so or not, what usually appears to be "reality" is experience which it appears that we share with other people. We check the content and qualities of our experience with the experience of others to see whether ours is "real" or not. With some orders of experience we check so automatically that it never occurs to us to ask whether we ought to, whether it is valid to check with others. When doubt strikes us with regard to the commonness of most experience, we fear we may be retreating from reality into fantasy.

And of course it is in the areas of experience which are most socially verifiable that we feel ourselves most shared and sharing. In a game the ball is either caught or not caught—and the resultant exultation or dejection depends altogether on group-related gambling emotions. The like holds true for the law or politics; they also entirely depend on community of experience, on the experience of reality as common vision.

So it is just upon this question of the possibility of experience socially based upon common vision that the possibility of literary realism hangs. If the novelist can through the illusions of his art induce imaginative experience within his reader consonant with the reader's ordinary communal experience, then intriguing possibilities appear. There can be a literature peculiarly potent in its appeal to some of the sanest and most useful processes of the human mind. From certain practical and moral points of view, that should be a literature uniquely valuable—for, if it were successful as art, done with esthetic force, conceived by the eye of a necessarily supersensitive observer, the illusion of experience, the "sense of life" conveyed could not fail to be deeply instructive. The power of art to create experience more intense, more sharply defined and vivid, more satisfactorily shaped than the experience people can normally create for themselves would be lent to the deepening and enhancement of the common vision. Such literature would make us better citizens, more loyal in our loves, more perceptive in critique, more faithful to perspectives clearly seen.

Such a literature would be time and culture bound of course. Especially concerned with persons in their relations with other persons, it would tend to be democratic. In order to preserve its integrity as art rather than essay or sermon, it would have to forswear the vatic anarchies of "organicism" and concentrate hard on problems of form. It would learn to master the arts of creating illusions of objectivity and impartiality, abjuring the cult of artistic personality and the temptation to romantic irony.

All these, and perhaps other, features would go to make a particular kind of literary method and effect. The importance of the kind would, as with all kinds, depend largely on the power of its practitioner to achieve artistic success—the strong command of the reader's imagination—by its method. In this respect the kind would be no different from any other. The whole argument here is to show that the literary art of the common vision deserves recognition as a kind and is, theoretically as well as historically, entitled to the name of realism.

CHAPTER 2

The Rise of Naturalism

American
Realism

The Biological Model: Darwin, Zola, and American Naturalism

Richard Lehan

Richard Lehan views American Naturalism in the context of the scientific ideas of Charles Darwin, and the philosophy of literature put forward by French novelist and social critic Émile Zola. Lehan recounts some central facts of mid-nineteenth century Europe that Zola wrote about: the shift in population from the land to the city that accompanied industrialization, the growing gap between the wealthy and the poor, and the growing alienation of individuals from modern society. Adopting the theories of evolution and natural selection central to Darwin's discoveries, Zola's novels viewed society with the same objectivity and detached analysis that one associates with a scientific experiment. Lehan illustrates how the social and economic changes that characterized Europe in the 1850s and 1860s occurred in America in the 1880s and 1890s. Correspondingly, two of America's best Naturalist writers, Theodore Dreiser and Frank Norris, transplanted Darwin and Zola's ideas and put them to effective use in analyzing American society. Richard Lehan is an Emeritus Professor of English at the University of California at Los Angeles. He has written extensively on F. Scott Fitzgerald and Theodore Dreiser. His most recent work is *The City in Literature: An Intellectual and Cultural History.*

Literary naturalism derives mainly from a biological model. Its origin owes much to Charles Darwin and his theory of evolution, based in turn on his theory of natural selection. Darwin created a context that made naturalism—with its emphasis upon theories of heredity and environment—a

Excerpted from "The European Background," by Richard Lehan, in *The Cambridge Companion to American Realism and Naturalism: Howells to London,* edited by Donald Pizer. Copyright ©1995 by the Cambridge University Press. Reprinted with permission from the Cambridge University Press.

convincing way to explain the nature of reality for the late nineteenth century. But before Darwin's ideas were available in literary form, they had to be transformed by Emile Zola in his *Le Roman expérimental* (1880). Zola, in turn, based his theories of heredity and environment on Prosper Lucas's *Traité . . . de l'hérédité naturelle* (1850) and especially Claude Bernard's *Introduction à l'étude de la médicine expérimentale* (1865). Zola believed that the literary imagination could make use of the ideas in these books so long as the novelist functioned like a scientist, observing nature and social data, rejecting supernatural and transhistorical explanations of the physical world, rejecting absolute standards of morality and free will, and depicting nature and human experience as a deterministic and mechanistic process. All reality could be explained by a biological understanding of matter, subject to natural laws, available in scientific terms. Controlled by heredity and environment, man was the product of his temperament in a social context. "I wanted to study temperaments and not character," Zola wrote. "I chose beings powerfully dominated by their nerves and their blood, devoid of free will, carried away by the fatalities of their flesh."

THE PESSIMISM AND OPTIMISM OF NATURALISM

Zola gave his contemporaries a totally new way of thinking about the novel. Temperament was more important than character; setting could not be separated from a naturalistic theory of environment, nor plot from theories of evolution. Man was in a halfway house between the realm of the animals and some more perfect realm of being which future development would reveal. While the naturalistic novel often deals with a static moment in time, it also presupposes an atavistic[1] past or a futuristic ideal toward which characters can be drawn. The futuristic plots move toward forms of science fiction and utopian fantasy; the atavistic, toward dystopia and the animalistic, often the monstrous, although in some naturalistic narratives (for example, Jack London) this pull away from civilization and decadence toward the more savage sometimes brings with it a lost vitality. But, on the whole, such movement toward a more primitive self is destructive, as we see in Frank Norris's *McTeague*. Thus, while the naturalistic novel presumes the reality of evolu-

1. primitive

tion, it often works in terms of devolution: degeneration and personal decline are embedded in most naturalistic fiction. And such decay finds its equivalence on the social level, where the fate of the individual is often inseparable from a declining family or the new urbanized crowd. The crowd, more than just an aggregate of individuals, has a reality of its own and is capable of bestial and violent behavior, mindlessly following a leader, whose own fate at the hands of the mob can be extremely tenuous. (Contained in this aspect of literary naturalism is an anticipation of fascism and forms of totalitarianism.) We see these elements at work in such Zola novels as *Nana* and *Germinal,* where the corruption of the individual finds a natural correspondence in the corruption of the family and society itself. Everything is corrupt and capable of degeneration and debasement, from the highest orders of government and the salon to the workers in the mines and the people in the street.

And yet naturalism, while admittedly pessimistic, seems to have an optimistic element built into it. This stems from the usually unexpressed belief that whereas the fate of the individual is circumscribed and destined to end in sickness and death, the fate of the species is to move ever onward and upward in an evolutionary march toward greater perfection. Although these ideas are implicit in Darwin, they were made explicit by Herbert Spencer, one of Darwin's most influential interpreters. Literary naturalism thus had two images of man competing within it. A good many of the later naturalists projected a more highly evolved man in our future (for example, H.G. Wells's *Invisible Man)* at the same time as they showed how debased man could become if moved back in evolutionary time (Wells's *The Island of Dr. Moreau).*

NATURALISM'S DEPARTURE FROM THE ROMANCE

One of the major differences between literary naturalism and the romance fiction which preceded it is that naturalism moved us away from the distant historical past to the more immediate historical present. More contemporary problems were foregrounded in naturalism. Zola, for example, whose writing career spanned the years 1870–90, concentrated on the years of the [French] Second Empire (1851–70). Every one of his novels dealt with a topical issue of these times: the greed for land of the peasantry, the movement of the peasantry from the land to the city, the fate of the urban worker, the corruption of the high-society prostitute, the rise of the department store, the function of the urban market, the fate of the new industrial worker, the rise of the steam engine and railroad system, the fate of a degenerating France as it prepared for war with Germany. Zola's influence on his contemporaries was pronounced, perhaps more so in America than in Europe. Although Theodor Fontane and Gerhart Hauptmann wrote naturalistic novels in Germany, and George Moore and George Gissing in England, the real inheritors of the method were American writers like Frank Norris, Theodore Dreiser, and Jack London. . . .

DARWIN AND ZOLA

Darwinism was both a continuation of and a challenge to Enlightenment assumptions. As a theory of evolution, it revealed the physical process of the universe, matter unfolding in time. But as a theory of natural selection—that species change through a process of adaptation to their immediate environment—Darwinism emphasized the accidental rather than a necessary unfolding, seriously challenging the notion of design. Darwin's theory of evolution contained the idea of devolution and degeneration. Natural selection argues that the best in the species are attracted to and mate with each other. This leaves the worst in the species to mate and generate their own offspring. Literary naturalism gave far more attention to such evolutionary throwbacks than to its forward progress—a fact easily seen in the *Rougon-Macquart* novels of Zola. . . .

Zola believed that the same forces which determined the individual were at work in society. The naturalist's view of the individual, the family, and the crowd had a logical correspondence in culture and in history itself. It oversimplifies to say that Zola believed that the life lived closest to nature was good, the life lived closest to society bad, although at times this would seem to be the case. What Zola was suggesting was something slightly different—namely, that modern man had been displaced from anything like a natural environment, had lost contact with his instincts and a more rudimentary and basic sense of self, and had become more and more distanced from the rhythms of the natural life. Money and bureaucracy had replaced the workings of nature and natural feelings.

Ironically, as civilization became more and more pronounced, society became more and more corrupt. Zola believed that beneath all the trappings society was a festering mass of infected sores. At the center of this situation was Louis Napoleon and the Second Empire. In 1848 Napoleon replaced Louis Philippe as president of France, betrayed that office on 2 December 1851 when his troops took control of Paris, and abandoned the idea of the republic a year later when he became Napoleon III, emperor of the Second Empire, with a new constitution of 14 January 1853 codifying his powers. On the surface, this event was not without benefits: canals and rivers were dug and widened, giving France one of the best transportation systems in Europe. Baron Georges-Eugène Haussmann (1809–91) was hired to remove medieval and build modern Paris. Haussmann demolished 20,000 slum dwellings and built 43,777 new homes, lengthened the rue de Rivoli from the Bastille to the Concorde, and built the boulevards Saint-Michel, Sébastopol, Strasbourg, and Magenta. The Saint-Martin canal was covered and turned into a boulevard. The Bois de Boulogne and Vincennes were made into public parks, and a new symmetry made such buildings as the Louvre, the Hôtel de Ville, the Palais Royal, the National Library, Notre Dame, and the Opéra into monuments. Paris became the center of Europe, with six great railroad lines converging on the capital. Under Napoleon III new credit lines were established by two lending institutions: the Crédit Mobilier handled mainly industrial loans; the Crédit Financier, mostly agrarian ones. Money transformed the new city from within and without; Paris and other cities became a magnet for those in the provinces. In the time of Napoleon's reign, Paris almost doubled in population, while such cities as Lyons, Marseilles, Bordeaux, and Lille became urban centers. . . .

On the level of the individual, Zola's frame of reference was biological; on the level of society, his frame of reference was the land. Although all realists do not start from the same assumptions, realism/naturalism as a literary movement depended upon showing how a new commercial/industrial process had interrupted the old rhythms of the land and put in motion a social process that was more often than not culturally destructive.

AMERICAN TRANSFORMATIONS OF DARWIN AND ZOLA

The question that now confronts us is that of whether or not European realism/naturalism had an American equivalent.

No one can deny a connection between (say) Zola and Norris and Balzac[2] and Dreiser, but what is the nature of this connection? What often goes unnoticed in this discussion is the fact that Norris and Dreiser shared a historical moment with Balzac and Zola: all these novelists were setting their novels in a world growing more and more industrial. In fact, one could argue that the aftermath of the Civil War in America paralleled the kind of historical change taking place in France between 1848 and 1870, as both economies moved from a landed to a commercial/industrial world. In America, this period witnessed the rapid growth of cities, the rise of corporate businesses, the influx of immigrant labor, and the practice of wretched working conditions. As in Zola, we can move, in the American postbellum novels, from the boardrooms of power and wealth to the salons where the wealth is displayed, to the legislative forums that the wealth controls, to the mills, factories, and mines that produce the wealth at great human sacrifice and suffering. The question of cultural conditioning, however, can take the discussion only so far. And the question of direct literary influence is even more limiting in the discourse of recent criticism: literary works are too complex to "derive" from any one source. But Zola did more than write several dozen novels: he also gave rise to a narrative methodology, a way of seeing reality, that left its mark on both sides of the Atlantic.

FRANK NORRIS'S NATURALISM

And, like those of Zola, Frank Norris's and Theodore Dreiser's novels (in different ways) take their being from a naturalistic biology. Characters like McTeague and Vandover are very much a product of an animality that leads to decline and degeneration, especially when their more debased instincts are stimulated by alcohol and profligacy. McTeague tries to fight off the beast within him: his resolve wavers for a moment when he has Trina helpless under the influence of gas in his dentist chair. But it is not until his office is shut down and he is thrown onto the street that he falls under the destructive influence of alcohol, which accelerates the degenerative process. Poverty has the same erosive affect on Trina and McTeague that it has on Gervaise and Coupeau in [Zola's] *L'Assommoir*, and it brings to the surface the same

2. French novelist Honoré de Balzac was considered the earliest master of French realism.

homicidal tendencies that we see in Jacques Lantier in [Zola's] *La Bête humaine*. What we see in Norris is the biology of greed, a desire for money and gold so extreme that it can create an illusionary reality and pathology of murder.

The same kind of extreme pathology also applies to Vandover. A graduate of Harvard University, he is protected by the money and social status his father provides. When his father dies and he is being sued for his part in the death of Ida Wade, he begins to drink more intemperately and to gamble with reckless abandon. Vandover's decline involves physical and mental sickness, a form of lycanthropy, in which he feels that he is becoming a wolf. As in Zola, the animal condition exists in us as a potential state to be aroused at moments of physical and emotional crisis, and the rise of this animality is always followed by a process of degeneration. The last we see of Vandover, he is destitute, derelict, and sick, cleaning the muck out of one of Charles Geary's rental homes. Such debris is the equivalent of the junk we see in Zerkow's junk shop in *McTeague*. Society is continuously breaking down, throwing away its waste, rubbish, and junk, including the human jetsam that makes up this world. There is always an ongoing process of death and renewal, a life force driving ahead of us, carrying the Charles Gearys to greater heights and the Vandovers and McTeagues to their deaths.

Norris's unfinished trilogy involving the story of wheat was his attempt to show how capitalism had created a world city based upon the principles of biology. While Norris's sympathy in *The Octopus* was clearly against the railroad and with the ranchers, he showed how the ranchers were also corrupted by money, how they exploited the land for immediate gain, and how they were also leaving a legacy of greed, bribery, and deceitful influence. There were no innocents in this economic process—only the working of the wheat, embodying the great force of nature itself. What used to be a symbiotic relationship between city and countryside has broken down; the city feeds off the land and depletes without restoring. Like Zola, Norris depicted the movement away from the land to the city, the wheat as a force in itself, now handled as an abstraction, being funneled through the city to markets all over the world. In his next novel, *The Pit* (1903), Norris further developed this theme, convincingly showing Chicago as a center into and out of which energy flowed: Chicago was a "force" that "turned the wheels of a harvester and seeder a thousand miles distant in Iowa and Kansas," the "heart of America," a force of empire that determined "how much the peasant [in Europe] shall pay for his loaf of bread." But as central as Chicago and wheat speculation are to Norris's story, the wheat is an even greater force, larger than both. Norris depicts a world of limits, and when Jadwin tries to raise the price of wheat beyond its limit, the market breaks and he is a ruined man. Every man and every social institution has its limit, and even abstract matters like wheat speculation are governed by laws that ultimately come back to nature—the land, the wheat, and the forces out of which life germinates—a theme Norris shared with Zola. Norris never finished the third volume of his story about wheat, never got to Europe where the consumption of wheat would be the final step in the cycle of life. But thematically a third volume was unnecessary: Norris had already shown how the growing and selling of wheat touches the lives of everyone worldwide, and he had clearly documented the biological basis of economics and the process of degeneration that can occur when one is no longer in touch with the rhythms of the land.

THEODORE DREISER'S NATURALISM

A process of degeneration is also central to the novels of Theodore Dreiser. His novels make use of the cycle of life, the rise and fall of human energies. The story of Hurstwood's decline is counterpointed by the story of Carrie's rise. Throughout, life is combat. Beneath the calm appearance of civilized life is a struggle as deadly as that of the jungle. The metaphor of animals at war runs through his novels. Dreiser begins his *The Financier* with the famous description of the lobster consuming the squid. Men devour the lobster in turn. But who preys on men? Cowperwood puzzles before the answer comes: they prey on each other. Self-interest and self-aggrandizement belie the institutions of law and justice. The ultimate truth is biological: the battle is to the cunning and the strong. As Dreiser begins *The Financier* with a metaphor, he also ends it with one: that of the Black Grouper, a fish of 250 pounds which can adapt perfectly to its surroundings, change its color, and prey upon the unsuspecting.

In *The Financier*, Dreiser emphasizes the obsessive nature of Cowperwood, who early in life decides to be a moneymaker, and shows how the genius for this work is a matter of temperament, built into his nature. But like Zola and Norris,

Dreiser saw that the economic process had its origin in nature; that, like a vast biological system, what happened in one realm rippled into another. When the Franco-Prussian War tied up European capital, Cooke's house failed—just as the Chicago fire of 1871 brought ruin to Cowperwood. In *The Titan,* Cowperwood's acquisitiveness engenders a swarm of wary but powerful enemies who finally overthrow him, just as the lead dog in a pack earns the respect and the enmity of those it displaces. All naturalistic fiction takes place in a quantifiable world of forces—with the exception of the life force—that eventually cancel each other out. Zola's and Dreiser's characters have moments . . . when they intuit these biological secrets. Such understanding brings with it an awe of the mysterious workings of life, but those most sensitive to such meaning often fall victim to ideals or illusions, miscalculate the mechanistic meaning of reality, and perish in a disillusionment that often brings on physical decline. Such is the fate of Claude Lantier in *L'Oeuvre;* such also is Cowperwood's fate. In naturalistic fiction, once one dreams oneself out of tune with nature, the results are often fatal.

In *The Financier* and *The Titan,* Dreiser defined more clearly than ever before the biological and mechanistic nature of social reality: man is just once removed from the animals. A creative force talks through him in the form of "temperament." He lives by strength and cunning in a society of illusions, which upholds absolute justice and Christian restraint while the forces of greed, trickery, and self-interest work corruptingly, and in deadly combat, out of view. Like all men, weak or strong, Cowperwood demonstrated the nature of man in motion—a fury of activity, struggling, plotting, tricking—all heading nowhere but the grave. And yet—hungry for experience, power, love, beauty—he lived. Life is its own justification; the mad race goes in a strange circle; but to have lived is nothing and all. In the Cowperwood story, Dreiser was writing directly out of the naturalistic narrative mode: man's nature is fixed, the strong and the sly win for a time, all combat is eventually destructive, and life cancels itself out and then begins again—and this mysterious process is its own justification.

TOWARD A DEFINITION OF NATURALISM

We can now return to some of the questions with which we began—such as, is there a literary naturalism? The answer,

I have argued, is yes, if we mean by this a spectrum of ideas controlled by a literary method but used variously by a group of writers who brought the doctrine into being. But the answer is no, if we mean by this a coherent and self-sustained doctrine uniformly used by the same group of writers. Perhaps we can best avoid confusion by thinking of literary naturalism as involving a *synoptic* text—that is, a text similar to the three books of the New Testament that have elements in common at the same time as each text preserves its own uniqueness and difference. As a narrative mode, literary naturalism has a beginning and an end, a European origin and a multinational history. As we have seen, it depends upon a biological model, relying heavily on theories of evolution and devolution, seeing man as a product of his immediate environment. It is essentially mechanistic in its view of matter and deterministic in its attitude toward human will, moving toward theories of degeneration when viewing the individual, the family, the crowd, and finally the community itself, whether it be the city or the nation-state. As a narrative mode, literary naturalism involved a way of seeing. It rested upon the scientific assumption that history can be documented and the mind functions empirically. The naturalistic novel usually involved a double perspective: one point of view, delimited and incomprehensive, involved that of the characters who had little sense of the meaning of the world around them; the other was the more expansive view of the author or narrative commentator, which alerted the reader to the crises about to befall the characters. The two views resulted in the narrative irony that is the benchmark of naturalism—the constant play between what the characters anticipate and what the reader/narrator anticipate. As a literary way of presenting reality, naturalism dominated in Europe, especially in France, from 1870 to 1890, and in America from 1890 to the end of World War II.

The Dual Nature of Naturalism

Charles C. Walcutt

For Charles Walcutt, literary Naturalism was a complex movement that was both pessimistic and optimistic about human nature. On the one hand, the Naturalists saw life as an endless struggle. Individuals were viewed as prisoners of their biologically determined natures, prone at any time to lapses into an animal-like primitivism. On the other hand, the Naturalists adopted Darwin's idea of evolution, and believed that humankind was in a constant state of transition as it developed towards a state of perfection. These two impulses—this "divided stream" within literary naturalism—constitute the title of Walcutt's book. Charles Walcutt taught at Queens College in New York and at the Graduate Center of the City University of New York. His *American Literary Naturalism: The Divided Stream* (1956) remains one of the most significant works on Naturalism ever published.

Out of the never-resolved tension between the ideal of perfect unity and the brutal facts of experience come the themes, motifs, forms, and styles through which naturalism found literary expression. These are all part of the picture of naturalism, although some are there more or less by chance. To list them briefly is to suggest the rather disorderly composition of this picture.

NATURALISM'S THEMES

The major themes and motifs are *determinism, survival, violence,* and *taboo.* The theme of determinism, which is of course basic, carries the idea that natural law and socioeconomic influences are more powerful than the human will. The theme of survival grows out of the application of deter-

Excerpted from *American Literary Naturalism: A Divided Stream,* by Charles C. Walcutt. Copyright ©1956 by the University of Minnesota. Reprinted with permission from the University of Minnesota Press.

minism to biological competition; the notion that survival is the supreme motive in animal life provides a point of view from which all emotion, motivation, and conflict may be approached; it fastens man to his physical roots. The theme of violence grows with the transfer of emphasis from tradition (ultimately supernatural tradition) to survival. Animal survival is a matter of violence, of force against force; and with this theme there emerge various motifs having to do with the expression of force and violence and with the exploration of man's capacities for such violence. "The lower nature of man," in short, is revealed, explored, emphasized. It is also defiantly and triumphantly brandished; it may indeed be worshiped! A generation later this theme will be found to have modulated into the discovery of psychic recesses—the acknowledgment of new kinds and qualities of emotional experience. The last link in this chain, dangling from survival and violence, comes as an assault on taboo: a host of topics that had been considered improper—sex, disease, bodily functions, obscenity, depravity—were found to be in the province of physical survival. In that province, where the naturalists focused their attention, they could not be ignored. Nobody wanted to ignore them.

Naturalism's Forms

The forms which the naturalistic novel assumes are *clinical, panoramic, slice-of-life, stream of consciousness,* and *chronicle of despair.* When the idea of the free, responsible human will, making ethical choices that control its fate, is set aside in favor of such concepts as determinism and survival, a new notion of social process has appeared. It is dramatized (or enacted) in these new kinds of novels. Biological determinism can be set forth in a clinical study of disease or deterioration, in which the course of the malady or mania is traced step by step as it destroys the individual. When these forces operate in or through the whole body of society, a panoramic novel appears. Zola's *Germinal,* which "studies" a coal mining community and shows the miners helplessly squeezed to the edge of starvation by laissez-faire capitalism, is the classic of this form and the archetype of the proletarian novel. The minute and faithful reproduction of some bit of reality, without selection, organization, or judgment, every smallest detail presented with "scientific" fidelity, is the formless form of a slice-of-life novel. The same approach, but to the content of the mind (all the data of experience) rather than to external reality, gives a stream of consciousness novel, in which every smallest detail of thought is presented without selection, organization, or judgment. And finally there is the chronicle of despair, in which a whole life is depicted as the weary protagonist trudges across the dreary wastes of the modern world and finds, usually, an early death. . . .

The point is that naturalism involved a continual *search* for form. These are the forms it would have attained if its materialistic premises had been wholly and consistently followed. The fact that such premises were not—and probably could not have been—consistently maintained accounts for the complexity and fascination of literary naturalism as a problem. . . .

STYLES IN NATURALISM

Naturalistic styles cannot be defined in any exclusive sense. They can be listed, perhaps, as *documentary, satiric, impressionistic,* and *sensational;* but these are not very accurate terms for describing styles, and they are certainly not exclusive. The ideal of a fact-freighted, uncolored, objective, "scientific" style can be stated, but it is not easy to find an example of it in the novel. Frequently the most superficially objective or restrained style is the most highly charged with bitterness or indignation—as in the minute and faithful reproductions of stupid conversations by, say, James T. Farrell, or the vitriolic attacks on the middle class by contemporaries of de Maupassant in France. At the other extreme, the style of Zola, the fountainhead of naturalism, is recognized as highly romantic by all the critics, as is the style of his closest follower in America, Frank Norris, who went to considerable pains in one of his essays to explain that naturalism was romantic rather than realistic. In a "naturalistic" novel, where the subject matter is sensational, the style is likely to be restrained and objective; where the subject matter is commonplace, the style is likely to be turbulent or "romantic."

For these reasons, there cannot be a "naturalistic style." . . . The term *romantic,* in this connection, indicates an attitude or quality—an exuberance or intensity of approach, a sense of vitality or richness, a feeling that the demands of the human spirit cannot be met by the commonplace or typical occasions of life. This romantic quality is frequently achieved by naturalistic subject matter presented (because it is sensational) in a style that is restrained and objective; here the effect would be called romantic, whereas the style would be called realistic. Where the subject matter is typically romantic, as for example in Melville's *Typee*, the romantic effect is rendered through a realistic style. Realism in style is, as everyone knows, relative: the "realistic" Dickens style has been turned by the passage of years into what might today be called romantic. Even in our time, what was the poignant, intense realism of Hemingway in 1927 has come to be considered romantic and even . . . sentimental. When novels like Zola's *Germinal* and Norris's *McTeague* are considered naturalistic in philosophy, romantic in effect, and (though not consistently) realistic in style, it becomes very apparent that the three terms are not mutually exclusive; no one of them can characterize a novel to the exclusion of the other two. I use the term *naturalism* to indicate a philosophical orientation; *romanticism* to indicate extremes or intensities of effect; *realism* to indicate the apparent fidelity, through style, to details of objects, manners, or speech.

PROBLEMS IN DEFINING NATURALISM

The word *naturalistic*, then, labels a philosophy fairly adequately, but by the time we have passed through the varieties of social and ethical application that have been drawn from it and listed the forms, styles, and motifs that it has evoked, we dare speak of the "naturalistic" novel only with the reservations implied by quotation marks. The significant form of a novel cannot be deduced from the fact that its writer is a philosophical naturalist, for naturalism does not account for spirit, imagination, and personality. A work that was perfectly controlled by the theory of materialistic determinism would not be a novel but a report. It is not surprising, therefore, that critics have run aground or afoul of each other when they have tried to characterize the naturalistic novel with sweeping generalizations. Current theories about the nature of naturalism disagree in general and in detail. They disagree so fundamentally that they give diametrically contrary statements about the matter. The focus of discord seems to be the question of whether the naturalistic novel is "optimistic" or "pessimistic." Some critics insist that the essence of naturalism is "pessimistic determinism," expressing resignation or even despair at the spectacle of man's impotence in a mechanistic universe; others claim that the naturalistic novel is informed with a bright, cheerful, and vigorous affirmation of progress—of man's ability through science to control his environment and achieve Utopia.

The hostility of such points of view might lead one to expect that their proponents were writing about entirely different groups of books, but they are not. It is true that one writer excludes Dreiser from the naturalistic movement, whereas another finds its epitome in his work; but on the whole these antipodal camps are dealing with the same works. The cause of the discord lies in the relation between science and literature: specifically, in the idea that scientific attitudes produce equivalent aesthetic effects. . . .

THE CONFLICT BETWEEN ART AND SCIENCE

The key to this puzzle (for it can be solved) lies in a distinction between what the socially minded man thinks and what the work of art is. The scientist who wants to improve the lot of man through knowledge and manipulation of the material world faces two obstacles: lethargy and unbelief. Some people think mankind is doing well enough. Others do not think that anything can be accomplished with "human nature" by scientific methods. The scientist-reformer therefore has to establish the validity of two assumptions: that the state of man needs to be improved, and that human conditions are determined by the operation of material causes which can be traced, recorded, understood, and, finally, controlled. The pieces of the puzzle fall into place when we understand that the best possible way to illustrate and validate these two assumptions is to write a "naturalistic" tragedy in which a human being is crushed and destroyed by the operation of forces which he has no power to resist or even understand. The more helpless the individual and the more clearly the links in an inexorable chain of causation are defined, the more effectively documented are the two assumptions which underlie the scientists' program of reform, for the destruction of an individual demonstrates the power of heredity and environment over human destinies. And if the victim's lot is sordid, the need for reform is "proved." The more helpless the character, the stronger the proof of determinism; and once such a thesis is established the scientist hopes and believes that men will set about trying to control the forces which now control men.

Thus can the scientists' "optimistic" purpose be served by

a "pessimistic" novel; and thus we see how the deduction that both must be either optimistic or pessimistic is untrue. In the works of Zola we frequently see pictures of degeneration and depravity flourished with the enthusiasm of a sideshow barker describing a two-headed lady. The zeal is such that one imagines the author rubbing his hands in delight over his monsters. The most casual reading of *L'Assommoir* will identify this fusion of opposites—of sordid degeneracy and soaring enthusiasm—which troubles only the logical and abstracting critic.

DREISER'S *AN AMERICAN TRAGEDY*

The optimism of the scientist is undeniable; I shall not discuss here the formidable probability that it is not justified by his philosophy of naturalism. Nor do I mean to maintain that naturalistic novelists like Zola and Frank Norris grasped the distinction between a social policy, which proposes action, and a work of art, which is essentially self-contained. There is, on the contrary, a sharp discrepancy between what Zola announced in *Le Roman Expérimentale* and what he performed in his novels; it corresponds to the discrepancy between Theodore Dreiser's socialism and the inexorable fatality that controls *An American Tragedy.* Returning for a moment to our optimism-pessimism dilemma, we should not be surprised to find the critic who proceeds from social theory to literary practice affirming that *An American Tragedy* is authentic naturalism because Dreiser suggests that "radical social reforms are imperative"; whereas another might deduce, if he proceeded from the novel to the social theory, that the philosophy of naturalism is grimly pessimistic because the protagonist of the novel is utterly helpless to control his fate. But I should say that the novel is an almost ideal example of naturalism because within its framework Dreiser makes no proposals. He shows how, given certain hereditary and environmental conditions, what did happen had to happen; and he communicates this conviction because he is able to present so detailed an account of events that Clyde Griffiths is shown as powerless to choose at the very climax of the action and is never held morally responsible for his "crime."

Within its aesthetic frame the novel is completely deterministic and might be called pessimistic . . . it is for this reason that it can be considered an unusually consistent (and

powerful) expression of the naturalistic philosophy. No
novel, of course, can actually render the total context of an
event. But it can create the *illusion* of doing so; and this is the
fundamental aim, as well as the criterion, of this type of naturalistic novel. The writer's opinions about social justice
cannot and will not interfere with the form of the work.

Observing the operation of determinism in *An American
Tragedy*, the reader may well be led to conclude that something should be done to change the conditions that produce
such tragedies. But this happens to the reader, not in the
novel; and I believe it can be shown that it happens after and
apart from the aesthetic experience of the novel, although of
course it is an effect of the book and undoubtedly the author's intention. The force of this social conclusion depends,
paradoxically, on the very inexorable fatality of the action.
The ultimate social implications of the action are doubtless
with the reader as he reads, too, since no man can stay constantly within the framework or be constantly and exclu-
sively controlled by the assumptions of the work he is reading; indeed his awareness of social conditioning and of the
effect of social and financial ambition on Clyde Griffiths is
an important element in his awareness that the work of art
which he contemplates is unique and self-contained. The
conditions as given are absolute for Clyde, although for
America they can be improved. Reading a naturalistic
tragedy in which the hero appears to have no freedom, one
can know that one is performing an act of freedom in reading the book, and can sense that the author is by no means
contained by the determinism which controls his novel, for
he appeals to the reader's freedom and idealism as he shows
that his hero is trapped. Thus the heightening of the reader's
social consciousness (and any impulse to social action
which he may subsequently experience) comes precisely
because the movement of *An American Tragedy* is so perfectly "fatalistic," presenting in its massive and lumbering
fashion a superb integration of structure and underlying
philosophy. Observing this, the reader enjoys an access of
wisdom that would not come if he were being systematically
exhorted to action.

But *can* anything but despair emerge from such a spectacle? And by what right do we call a naturalistic novel tragic,
when its premises strip the protagonist of will and ethical
responsibility? The answer lies, surely, in the fact that will is

not really absent from the naturalistic novel. It is, rather, taken away from the protagonist and the other characters and transferred to the reader and to society at large. The reader acknowledges his own will and responsibility even as he pities the helpless protagonist. But the protagonist is not an automaton: his fall is a tragic spectacle because the reader participates in it and feels that only by a failure of his will and the will of society could it have taken place. What appears as an error of choice or a weakness of character in the plays of Aeschylus and Shakespeare is thus transferred to society in the naturalistic tragedy; society has destroyed the hero and thus has destroyed a part of its immortal self— and pity and guilt result. It is guilt instead of terror, because the social forces which crush a hero are finally subject to man's will and do not have the fatal power and mystery of cosmic forces. This curious wrenching of the novel's enclosing frame, which permits the "guilty" reader to enter the action, explains, in part, why so much criticism of naturalism has dealt with the problem of social intent. It also shows that the Aristotelian definition of tragedy[1] is so fundamentally true that even a writer who believes he denies its premises nevertheless contrives to fulfill its conditions. If we can admit that *An American Tragedy* is tragic in this quasi-Aristotelian sense, we can take a further step and conclude that it is irrelevant to ask whether it is optimistic or pessimistic. The question is whether it is true. . . .

THE DIVIDED STREAM

When we grant that a novelist may promote his ideas on social reform by writing a novel in which he seeks to embody a thorough-going materialistic determinism, we evoke two formidable objections. First, carried through to perfection, such a work would be a report, uncolored by ideas of human personality or recognition of the freedom of the human spirit. Such a work does not exist as a novel, and one would be fairly safe in affirming that it could not exist and be a novel. Second, the conflict between confidence in progress-through-human-effort and a belief in scientific determinism is not reconciled by my showing that "tragic" novels can

---

1. Ancient Greek philosopher Aristotle defined tragedy as a drama that involved a dramatic fall from fortune by a character worthy of both fear and pity. The wide spectrum of responses drawn from an audience by this tragic character leads, according to Aristotle, to a purification of emotions and a profound insight into human nature.

document social optimism. The conflict remains. It is the chief problem that any "naturalistic" novel presents to a thoughtful reader. . . . Like the critical controversy over optimism and pessimism, it is evidence of the divided stream— of a profound uncertainty as to whether science liberates the human spirit or destroys it. Novels, novelists, and critics consistently reflect this modern tension between science as god and science as devil, between progress and despair, between the hope of the future and the values of the past, between the two faces of human and physical nature.

A final observation on these contradictions: Naturalistic fiction which purports to receive its sanction from the scientific method and deterministic philosophy usually reveals, to the dispassionate observer, affiliations with several aspects of the aesthetic of ugliness, and these are apt to play a larger part in the novel's form than may appear to us if we keep our attention too closely on such concepts as science and reform. Art is anthropocentric. It is created by men whose dominant concern is to domesticate the physical universe to the uses of man's spirit. This aim is accomplished—or approached—by the artist's attempts to impose patterns of human thought upon the endless and eternal complexity of the physical universe. No matter how ardently he appears to be denying the worth or importance of man, the autonomy of the will, the permanence of life, the value of man's spirit, or the power of his knowledge, he is always in some fashion affirming these very things, for art is exercise and proof of them. The naturalistic novelist while he portrays with loathing and bitterness the folly and degradation of man is also affirming his hope and his faith, for his unspoken strictures imply an equally unspoken ideal which stimulates and justifies his pejorative attitude toward the world about him. The act of criticism, furthermore, is an exercise of creative intelligence which in itself denies what it may be saying about the futility of life and the folly of man.

This denial is a term in the dialectic of art; it is as much a part of the total effect of the work of art as its stated or implied scientific hypothesis. Hence all "naturalistic" novels exist in a tension between determinism and its antithesis. The reader is aware of the opposition between what the artist says about man's fate and what his saying it affirms about man's hope. Both of these polar terms are a part of the "meaning" of a naturalistic novel.

Naturalism in Three Classic American Novels

Donald Pizer

Naturalist fiction has often been accused of being overly programmatic. Too often, according to critics, Naturalist plots and characters rigidly conform to a deterministic view of the world, where individuals become victims of either their more primitive desires, or social forces beyond their control. Donald Pizer argues that Naturalism is not as reductive as critics accuse it of being. While certainly adopting the theories of Darwin and Zola, among others, to produce a more scientifically objective and deterministic kind of fiction, Pizer illustrates the unique combination of the sensational and the commonplace in such classic Naturalist novels as *McTeague, Sister Carrie,* and *The Red Badge of Courage.* According to Pizer these authors give their characters, and the society in which they live, a dignity and complexity that proves beyond any doubt the worth of Naturalist fiction. Donald Pizer has taught for many years at Tulane University, and he is the author and editor of numerous books on American Realism and Naturalism.

The naturalistic novel is . . . not so superficial or reductive as it implicitly appears to be in its conventional definition. It involves a belief that life on its lowest levels is not so simple as it seems to be from higher levels. It suggests that even the least significant human being can feel and strive powerfully and can suffer the extraordinary consequences of his emotions, and that no range of human experience is free of . . . moral complexities and ambiguities. . . . Naturalism reflects an affirmative ethical conception of life, for it asserts the value of all life by endowing the lowest character with emo-

Excerpted from *The Theory and Practice of American Literary Naturalism,* by Donald Pizer (Carbondale, IL: Southern Illinois University Press, 1993). Reprinted with permission from the Associated University Presses.

tion and defeat and with moral ambiguity, no matter how poor or ignoble he may seem. The naturalistic novel derives much of its aesthetic effect from these contrasts. It involves us in the experience of a life both commonplace and extraordinary, both familiar and strange, both simple and complex. It pleases us with its sensationalism without affronting our sense of probability. It discovers the "romance of the commonplace," as Frank Norris put it. Thus, the melodramatic sensationalism and moral "confusion" that are often attacked in the naturalistic novel should really be incorporated into a normative definition of the mode and be recognized as its essential constituents.

The three novels that I have chosen to illustrate this definition, and also to suggest the possible range of variation within it, are Frank Norris's *McTeague* (1899), Theodore Dreiser's *Sister Carrie* (1900), and Stephen Crane's *The Red Badge of Courage* (1895)....

PASSIONATE DEPTHS BENEATH EVERYDAY SURFACES

A central theme in Norris's work is that beneath the surface of our placid, everyday lives there is turbulence, that the romance of the extraordinary is not limited to the distant in time and place but can be found "in the brownstone house on the corner and in the office building downtown." Norris therefore used the incident that had stimulated him to write the novel, a vicious murder in a San Francisco kindergarten, as a controlling paradox in *McTeague* as in scene after scene he introduces the sensational into the commonplace activities and setting of Polk Street. So we have such incidents as McTeague grossly kissing the anesthetized Trina in his dental parlor, or the nearly murderous fight between Marcus and McTeague at the picnic. Some of the best moments in the novel powerfully unite these two streams of the commonplace and the extraordinary. In one such moment the frightened and incoherent Trina, having just found Maria's corpse with its cut throat and its blood-soaked clothes, rushes out into the everyday routine of Polk Street and has difficulty convincing the butcher's boy that something is wrong or even convincing herself that it is not improper "to make a disturbance and create a scene in the street."

Norris believed that the source of this violence beneath the surface placidity of life is the presence in all men of animal qualities that have played a major role in man's evolutionary development but which are now frequently atavistic and destructive. Norris's theme is that man's racial atavism[1] (particularly his brute sexual desires) and man's individual family heritage (alcoholic degeneracy in McTeague's case) can combine as a force toward reversion, toward a return to the emotions and instincts of man's animal past. McTeague is in one sense a "special case" of reversion, since his atavistic brutality is in part caused by his degenerate parents. He is also, however, any man caught up in the net of sex, and in this second aspect of man's inherited animal nature Norris introduces a tragic element into McTeague's fall, an element that contributes to the novel's thematic tension.

SEX IN *MCTEAGUE*

In describing the courtship of Trina and McTeague, Norris is at pains to stress their overt sexual innocence yet intuitive sexuality. The woman in Trina "was not yet awakened; she was yet, as one might say, without sex." For McTeague, Trina is his "first experience. With her the feminine element suddenly entered his little world. It was not only her that he saw and felt, it was the woman, the whole sex, an entire new humanity." Despite their innocence and lack of experience, both react intuitively and atavistically—McTeague desiring to seize and possess her, she instinctively withdrawing yet desiring to be conquered.

The most important sexual encounter between McTeague and Trina occurs at the B Street Station where McTeague for a second time proposes. When Trina hesitates, he seizes her "in his enormous arms, crushing down her struggle with his immense strength. Then Trina gave up, all in an instant, turning her head to his. They kissed each other, grossly, full in the mouth." Within the literary conventions of the day, this kiss symbolizes Trina's sexual submission. At this moment the strands in the web of sexual determinism begin to pull taut, for "the instant she allowed him to kiss her, he thought less of her. She was not so desirable, after all." McTeague senses this diminution along with a dim awareness "that this must be so, that it belonged to the changeless order of things—the man desiring the woman only for what she withholds; the woman worshipping the man for that which she yields up to him. With each concession gained the

1. primitivism

man's desire cools; with every surrender made the woman's adoration increases." Norris is concerned in this second meeting not with a special flaw in McTeague or Trina but with a sexual determinism affecting all men. The possessive sexual desire of the man aroused by the first woman he experiences sensually, the instinctive desire of the woman for sexual submission responding to the first man who assaults her—these are the atavistic animal forces that bring Trina and McTeague together.

A major theme in *McTeague* is therefore that of the sexual tragedy of man and woman. Caught up by drives and instincts beyond their control or comprehension, they mate by chance. In *McTeague* sex is that which comes to all men and women, disrupting their lives and placing them in relationships that the sanctity of marriage cannot prevent from ending in chaos and destruction. Norris does not tell the old tale of the fallen fornicator, as he does in *Vandover and the Brute,* but rather reaches out toward the unexplored ground of the human dilemma of sexual attraction.

ARTISTIC TENSIONS IN *MCTEAGUE*

The tension between this deterministic aspect of *McTeague* and its humanistic element does not lie in McTeague as a fully developed tragic figure. Rather, it is contained in the theme that man can seldom escape the violence inherent in his own nature, that man's attempt to achieve an ordered world is constantly thwarted by man himself. Norris devotes much attention to the element of order in the details of McTeague's life not only because of his belief in the romance of the commonplace but because the destruction of that order is the source of the tragic quality in McTeague's fall and of our own compassionate involvement with him despite his grotesqueness. Norris carefully documents McTeague's life as a dentist and as an inhabitant of Polk Street because the habitual tasks and minor successes of this life represent the order and stability that McTeague requires. In the course of the novel we begin to feel compassion for him as he becomes a victim of Trina's avarice and as we recognize that his emerging brutality is at least partly the result of the destruction of his world. When McTeague learns that he can no longer practice dentistry, his reaction is that of a man whose life is emptied of all meaning. In a scene of considerable power Trina comes upon him sitting in his dental chair,

"looking stupidly out of the windows, across the roofs opposite, with an unseeing gaze, his red hands lying idly in his
lap." We are never completely one with McTeague; his brute
strength and dull mind put us off. But because he is trapped
in the universal net of sex, and because we recognize the
poignancy of the loss of his world, we respond to him ultimately as a human being in distress, as a figure of some significance despite his limitations—as a man, in short, whose
fall contains elements of the tragic. . . .

DESIRE IN *SISTER CARRIE*

Dreiser's central theme in *Sister Carrie,* however, sets forth
the idea . . . that the physically real is not the only reality
and that men seek something in life beyond it. His theme is
that those of a finer, more intense, more emotional nature
who desire to break out of their normal solid world—
whether it be a Carrie oppressed by the dull repetitiousness
and crudity of her sister's home, or a Hurstwood jaded by
the middle class trivialities of his family—that when such
as these strive to discover a life approximate to their natures
they introduce into their lives the violent and the extraordinary. Carrie leaves her sister's flat for two illicit alliances,
attracted to each man principally by the opportunities he offers for a better life. Drouet and Hurstwood represent to her
not so much wealth or sexual attraction as an appeal to
something intangibly richer and fuller in herself. She is
drawn to each in turn, and then finally to Ames, because
each appeals to some quality in her temperament that she
finds unfulfilled in her life of the moment. Dreiser's depiction of her almost asexual relations with all of these men
represents less his capitulation to contemporary publishing
restrictions (although some of this is present) than his desire that the three characters reflect the upward course of
Carrie's discovery and realization of her inner nature. Finally, Carrie's career on the stage symbolizes both the emotional intensity she is capable of bringing to life and the fact
that she requires the intrinsically extraordinary and excit-
ing world of the theater to call forth and embody her emotional depth. . . .

CHANCE AND NEED

Carrie, like many of Dreiser's characters, has her life shaped
by chance and need. Chance involves her with Drouet and

later plays a large role in Hurstwood's theft and therefore in her own departure with him. Her needs are of two kinds—first to attain the tangible objects and social symbols of comfort and beauty that she sees all around her in Chicago and New York, and then to be loved. Of the major forces in her life, it is primarily her desire for objects that furnish a sense of physical and mental well-being—for fine clothing and furniture and attractive apartments and satisfactory food—which determines much of her life. As she gains more of these, her fear of returning to poverty and crudity—to her sister's condition—impels her to seek even more vigorously. Much of the concrete world that Dreiser fills in so exhaustively in *Sister Carrie* thus exists as a determining force in Carrie's life, first moving her to escape it, as in her encounters with working-class Chicago, and then to reach out for it, as when Drouet takes her to a good restaurant and buys her some fashionable clothes and so introduces into her imagination the possibility of making these a part of her life.

But Carrie's response to her needs is only one side of her nature. She also possesses a quality that is intrinsic to her being, though its external shape (a Drouet, a dress seen on the street) is determined by accidental circumstance. For in this his first novel Dreiser endows Carrie with the same capacity to wonder and to dream that he felt so strongly in himself. It is this ability to dream about the nature of oneself and one's fate and of where one is going and how one will get there and to wonder whether happiness is real and possible or only an illusion—it is this capacity which ultimately questions the reality and meaning of the seemingly solid and plain world in which we find ourselves.

THE ROCKING CHAIR

This "dream" quality underlies the most striking symbol in the novel, the rocking chair. The rocking chair has correctly been interpreted as principally a symbol of circularity because Carrie rocks on her first night in Chicago and again at the novel's close in her New York apartment. Dreiser seems to imply by the symbol that nothing really has happened to Carrie, that although her outer circumstances have changed, she is essentially the same both morally and spiritually. The symbol does indeed function in this way, but it also, in its persistence, reflects Carrie's continuing ability to wonder about herself and her future and this reveals that her imaginative response to life has not been dulled by experience. Although she had not achieved the happiness that she thought accompanied the life she desired and which she now has, she will continue to search. Perhaps Ames represents the next, higher step in this quest, Dreiser implies. But in any case, she possesses this inner force, a force which is essentially bold and free. Although it brings her worry and loneliness—the rocking chair symbolizes these as well—it is an element in her that Dreiser finds estimable and moving. She will always be the dreamer, Dreiser says, and though her dreams take an earthly shape controlled by her world, and though she is judged immoral by the world because she violates conventions in pursuit of her dreams, she has for Dreiser—and for us, I believe—meaning and significance and stature because of her capacity to rock and dream, to question life and to pursue it. Thus Carrie seeks to fulfill each new venture and gain each new object as though these were the only realities of life, and yet by her very dissatisfaction and questioning of what she has gained to imply the greater reality of the mind and spirit that dreams and wonders. The rocking chair goes nowhere, but it moves, and in that paradox lies Dreiser's involvement with Carrie and his ability to communicate the intensity and nature of her quest. For in his mind, too, the world is both solid and unknowable, and man is ever pursuing and never finding.

THE ANTI-HEROISM OF *THE RED BADGE OF COURAGE*

The Red Badge of Courage also embodies a different combination of the sensational and commonplace than that found in *McTeague*. Whereas Norris demonstrates that the violent and the extraordinary are present in seemingly dull and commonplace lives, Crane, even more than Dreiser, is intent on revealing the commonplace nature of the seemingly exceptional. In *The Red Badge* Henry Fleming is a raw, untried country youth who seeks the romance and glory of war but who finds that his romantic, chivalric preconceptions of battle are false. Soldiers and generals do not strike heroic poses; the dead are not borne home triumphantly on their shields but fester where they have fallen; and courage is not a conscious striving for an ideal mode of behavior but a temporary delirium derived from animal fury and social pride or fear. A wounded officer worries about the cleanliness of his uniform; a soldier sweats and labors at his arms "like a laborer in a foundry"; and mere chance determines rewards and punishments—the death of a Conklin, the red badge of a Fleming. War to Crane is like life itself in its injustice, in its mixing of the ludicrous and the momentarily exhilarating, in its self-deceptions, and in its acceptance of appearances for realities. Much of Crane's imagery in the novel is therefore consciously and pointedly anti-heroic, not only in his obviously satirical use of conventional chivalric imagery in unheroic situations (a soldier bearing a rumor comes "waving his [shirt] bannerlike" and adopting "the important air of a herald in red and gold") but also more subtly in his use of machine and animal imagery to deflate potentially heroic moments.

Crane's desire to devalue the heroic in war stems in part from his stance as an ironist reacting against a literary and cultural tradition of idealized courage and chivalry. But another major element in his desire to reduce war to the commonplace arises from his casting of Fleming's experiences in the form of a "life" or initiation allegory. Henry Fleming is the universal youth who leaves home unaware of himself or the world. His participation in battle is his introduction to life as for the first time he tests himself and his preconceptions of experience against experience itself. He emerges at the end of the battle not entirely self-perceptive or firm-willed—Crane is too much the ironist for such a reversal—but rather as one who has encountered some of the strengths and some of the failings of himself and others. Crane implies that although Fleming may again run from battle and although he will no doubt always have the human capacity to rationalize his weaknesses, he is at least no longer the innocent.

THE COMMONPLACE AND THE SENSATIONAL

If *The Red Badge* is viewed in this way—that is, as an anti-heroic allegory of "life"—it becomes clear that Crane is representing in his own fashion the naturalistic belief in the interpenetration of the commonplace and the sensational. All life, Crane appears to be saying, is a struggle, a constant sea of violence in which we inevitably immerse ourselves and in which we test our beliefs and our values. War is an appropriate allegorical symbol of this test, for to Crane violence is the very essence of life, not in the broad Darwinian sense of a struggle for existence or the survival of the fittest, but rather in the sense that the proving and testing of oneself, conceived both realistically and symbolically, entails the violent and the deeply emotional, that the finding of oneself occurs best in moments of stress and is itself often an act of violence. To Crane, therefore, war as an allegorical setting for the emergence of youth into knowledge embodies both the violence of this birth and the commonplaces of life that the birth reveals—that men are controlled by the trivial, the accidental, the degradingly unheroic, despite the preservation of such accoutrements of the noble as a red badge or a captured flag. Crane shows us what Norris and Dreiser only suggest, that there is no separation between the sensational and the commonplace, that the two are coexistent in every aspect and range of life. He differs from Norris in kind and from Dreiser in degree in that his essentially ironic imagination leads him to reverse the expected and to find the commonplace in the violent rather than the sensational beneath the trivial. His image of life as an unheroic battle captures in one ironic symbol both his romanticism and his naturalism—or, in less literary terms, his belief that we reveal character in violence but that human character is predominantly fallible and self-deceptive. . . .

IRONY IN CRANE'S WORK

As was true of Norris and Dreiser, Crane's particular way of combining the sensational and the commonplace is closely related to the second major aspect of his naturalism, the thematic tension or complexity he embodies in his work. *The Red Badge* presents a vision of a man as a creature capable of advancing in some areas of knowledge and power but forever imprisoned within the walls of certain inescapable human and social imitations. Crane depicts the similarity between Henry Fleming's "will" and an animal's instinctive response to crisis or danger. He also presents Fleming's discovery that he is enclosed in a "moving box" of "tradition and law" even at those moments when he believes himself capable of rational decision and action—that the opinions and actions of other men control and direct him. Lastly, Crane dramatizes Fleming's realization that although he can project his emotions into natural phenomena and therefore derive comfort from a sense of nature's identification with his desires and needs, nature and man are really two, not one, and nature offers no reliable or useful guide to experience or to action. But, despite Crane's perception of these limitations and inadequacies, he does not paint a totally bleak picture of man in *The Red Badge.* True, Fleming's own sanguine view of himself at the close of the novel—that he is a man—cannot be taken at face value. Fleming's self-evaluations contrast ironically with his motives and actions throughout the novel, and his final estimation of himself represents primarily man's ability to be proud of his public deeds while rationalizing his private failings. . . .

THE RICHNESS OF AMERICAN NATURALISM

The primary goal of the late nineteenth-century American naturalists was not to demonstrate the overwhelming and oppressive reality of the material forces present in our lives. Their attempt, rather, was to represent the intermingling in life of controlling force and individual worth. If they were not always clear in distinguishing between these two qualities in experience, it was partly because they were novelists responding to life's complexities and were not philosophers categorizing experience, and partly because they were sufficiently of our own time to doubt the validity of moral or any other absolutes. The naturalists do not dehumanize man. They rather suggest new or modified areas of value in man while engaged in destroying such old and to them unreal sources of human self-importance as romantic love or moral responsibility or heroism. . . . One should not deny the bleak view of man inherent in McTeague's or Hurstwood's decline or in Fleming's self-deceptions, but neither should one forget that to the naturalists man's weaknesses and limited knowledge and thwarted desires were still sources of compassion and worth as well as aspects of the human condition to be more forthrightly acknowledged than writers had done in the past.

Nor is naturalism simply a piling on of unselective blocks of documentation. A successful naturalistic novel is like any successful work of art in that it embodies a cogent relationship between its form (its particular combination of the commonplace and sensational) and its theme (its particular tension between the individually significant and the deterministic). There is a major difference, within general similarities, between Norris's discovery of the sensational in the commonplace and Crane's dramatization of the triviality of the sensational. This variation derives principally from the differing thematic tension in the two novels. Norris wishes to demonstrate the tragic destruction of McTeague's commonplace world by the violence inherent in all life, whereas Crane wishes to dramatize Fleming's violent initiation into the commonplace nature of the heroic. Norris and Zane occupy positions in American naturalism analogous to that of Wordsworth and Byron in English romanticism. Like the poetry of the two earlier figures, their fiction expresses strikingly individual and contrasting visions of experience, yet does so within a body of shared intellectual and literary assumptions belonging to their common historical and literary moment.

CHAPTER 3

Class, Race, and Gender in American Realism

American
Realism

The Implications of Wealth in Two Realist Novels

Robert Shulman

Robert Shulman illustrates the extent to which Henry James's *The Portrait of a Lady* and William Dean Howells's *The Rise of Silas Lapham* reflect the complexities and anxieties of the Realist era. For Shulman, what defines and guides the psychology of the characters and so much of the action in these two novels is money. The desire to have more money, or the moral need to escape from the consequences of making and having money, mirrors the new culture of wealth that characterized America in the "Gilded Age." Typically, Henry James was often accused of being snobbish and removed from American life, while Howells has in retrospect been seen as an artlessly optimistic advocate of his time. Shulman takes issue with these judgments, and maintains that both Howells and James thoroughly analyzed the surfaces and hidden depths of American life after the Civil War. Robert Shulman is a Professor of English at the University of Washington. Besides editing a collection of Charlotte Perkins Gilman's stories and Owen Wister's novel *The Virginian*, he is the author of *Social Criticism and Nineteenth Century American Fictions* (1987).

For James's contemporaries, his *The Portrait of a Lady* (1881) was—and remains for us—an exemplary representative of American realism. Early in the book James describes the Archers' old double house in Albany and the full family life connected with it. James then carries Isabel Archer into the recesses of her childhood past and into the recesses of her favorite room, "a mysterious apartment" filled with old furniture with which "she had established relations almost human." The double house, the humanized room, and the sense of an inner life establish an intimate connection between house and self. Like the house, Isabel's self is divided or at least pulled in opposing directions. The door to the mysterious room is bolted, the door's sidelights are covered with green paper, and though as a little girl Isabel knew the door opened out onto the street "she had no wish to look out, for this would have interfered with her theory that there was a strange, unseen place on the other side—a place which became to the child's imagination, according to its different moods, a region of delight or of terror." Like the Emerson who celebrates the inner life of the self-sufficient individual, in this version Isabel looks inward into the depths of the imagination, creates a drama of delight or terror, and on principle avoids testing her theories against what she will find on "the vulgar street." As an adult in this same room she blithely tells her aunt, "I don't know anything about money." It is not really fair to equate Emerson, inwardness, and the imagination with the romantic and the street and money with realism. Emerson, after all, spoke for the meal in the firkin, the milk in the pan, and Isabel has an immense appetite for experience. In part James conceives Isabel so that he can explore a conflict between two sides of his American cultural heritage. As an American writer and realist, he is especially sensitive to the issue of the reliability of the imagination under the pressure of money and the vulgar street. . . .

MONEY IN *THE PORTRAIT OF A LADY*

In a possessive market society, money is the ultimate commodity, the ultimate possession. Isabel wants to see for herself, to judge for herself, but she does not know anything about money. She is also torn between her impulse to know the world, to throw herself into it, and her impulse to trust herself, to devalue worldly possessions, and to ignore the vulgar street. After she inherits a fortune, she is afraid. "A large fortune means freedom," she tells Ralph Touchett, "and I'm afraid of that." If she failed to make good use of it, she goes on, she "would be ashamed." The stakes are high because shame is intimately connected to a sense of personal identity and self-worth.

Isabel argues for a sense of self that excludes possessions. "Nothing that belongs to me," she tells Madame Merle, "is any measure of me; everything's on the contrary a limit, a barrier, and a perfectly arbitrary one." Isabel is particularly indifferent to houses and dress. Madame Merle disagrees. "What shall we call our 'self?'" she asks. "Where does it begin? where does it end? It overflows into everything that belongs to us—and then it flows back again. I know a large part of myself is the clothes I choose to wear. I've a great respect for *things!* One's self—or other people—is one's expression of one's self; and one's house, one's furniture, one's garments, the books one reads, the company one keeps— these things are all expressive." James has Madame Merle give a working definition of the self appropriate to an expanding consumer and possessive market society. On this view, the self expands or contracts in relation to possessions. "There's no such thing as an isolated man or woman," Madame Merle argues; "we're each of us made up of some cluster of appurtenances."

Until well after her marriage Isabel does not realize the extent to which Madame Merle and Osmond, two artists, two dramatists, have manipulated her. They present Osmond as a refined man indifferent to the opinion of the world, indifferent to money, indifferent to the "cluster of appurtenances." His relative poverty allows Isabel to feel generous. She is bestowing something on a worthy recipient. The power relations are the reverse of a marriage to either Lord Warburton or Caspar Goodwood. Osmond is also much less of a masculine sexual presence than either of his rivals. Isabel imagines a Gilbert Osmond and falls in love with her own creation. In the destabilizing crosscurrents of a changing market society, the imagination is both necessary and problematic. Isabel, committed to seeing for herself, is unable to see that Osmond worships money and the opinion of the vulgar society he professes to despise.

James tests and qualifies Isabel's view of the self and imagination. He probes the web of sexual and market society pressures that affect the way she sees. In a patrician green world apparently far removed from the vulgar street, James reveals that even for Isabel Archer, profit, money, and gain are at the center of her marriage, just as they have penetrated to the center of her self.

HOUSES AND SELVES

In James's version of psychological realism, he uses metaphoric language to take us deep into a character's consciousness. James repeatedly recognizes the intimate connection between houses and selves in a possessive market society, a relation that for him has moral, psychological, and sociopolitical implications. Isabel, for example, gradually becomes aware that in marrying Osmond she is being confined in a house of darkness, that she is being imprisoned in a mind that lets in no air or light, that is a dungeon. Osmond's hatred, contempt, and egotism are overwhelming. Isabel's terror builds. The imagery is dense and deep, as are Isabel's painful moral and psychological realizations. Rooted in American political culture, her concern with freedom and independence is as alive as her eventual sense that she has been turned into a commodity, another *objet d'art* for Osmond to add to his collection, like the antique Roman coin he meticulously copies. James does justice both to the gradual, oblique way the mind works and to Isabel's sudden flash of awareness as she watches the intimacy between the standing Madame Merle and the seated Gilbert Osmond. But for all his sensitivity to the inner workings of the mind, James's psychological probing is not privatized. James shows the relation between the inner self and the environing world of the vulgar street.

GREED, DECEPTION, AND "READING" THE WORLD

Ironically, under Osmond's fastidious surface, under the aspect of taste, he and Madame Merle come to embody money and the vulgar street. Through Madame Merle, James exposes not metaphysical evil but the socially constructed evil of a society that places money above everything. For profit Madame Merle, gifted, aware, and sensitive, nonetheless lies to and betrays her closest friends. "'I don't pretend to know what people are meant for,' said Madame Merle. 'I only know what I can do with them.'"

In a world where Osmond and Madame Merle are dominant forces, where their imagination, art, and dramatic skill are important, the world becomes a social text that may not be incomprehensible but that is also not easy to read. Osmond and Madame Merle embody the deception, manipulation of appearances, and obsession with profit that many social observers regard as basic to consumer capitalism. In his way Ralph is also manipulative but, as opposed to Osmond, Ralph is generous and loving. Ralph sees clearly that Osmond is a sterile dilettante who will grind Isabel in the mill of the conventional. Although he accurately reads the social text, Ralph is unable to prevent the marriage. Isabel comes to understand but the inner and outer obstacles are formidable. . . .

WILLIAM DEAN HOWELLS AND AMERICAN REALISM

As a critic and editor, [William Dean Howells] introduced advanced European realists like Émile Zola, Ivann Turgenev, Leo Tolstoy, and George Eliot to an American audience. He similarly made the case for contemporary American realists as diverse as John De Forrest and Mary E. Wilkins Freeman. He supported both Henry James and Mark Twain, "supported" as a friend, as a critic, and as an editor who published and paid for stories and novels. He also mediated between the American West and East, between Twain's vernacular world and the Boston of Emerson and the *Atlantic Monthly*. Deeply encoded in his career and fiction is Howells's complex involvement in the worlds of literary art and the publishing business. This is a particular instance of the larger tension facing all of those realists who were compelled to render both the surfaces and the underlying energies of the new America.

THE RISE OF SILAS LAPHAM

In *The Rise of Silas Lapham* (1885) Howells deals explicitly with the issues of realism and the morally threatening power of big money. He intertwines a series of stories centering on the ideal of self-sacrifice as this value emerges in the fictional sentimental novel *Tears, Idle Tears,* as it emerges in a love story within the novel *The Rise of Silas Lapham,* as it emerges in the story of the self-made millionaire, Silas Lapham, and as it emerges in the theory of realism of the minister, Mr. Sewall. Self-sacrifice is the cornerstone virtue of the nineteenth-century true woman. Howells exposes a false version of this ideal through *Tears, Idle Tears,* or *Slop, Silly Slop.* In this book the heroine sacrifices herself by giving up the man she loves because someone else has cared for him first. The details are realistic but the feelings and characters are "colossal" and of flattering "supernatural proportions." In contrast, the realistic novel championed by Howells and Mr. Sewall paints "life as it is and human feelings in their true proportions and relation." One test, then, is empirical, so that Howells looks at the world of experience, which in his practice is the world of middle-class America.

Another test is metaphysical, since Howells assumes that fi nally ordinary American life will confirm ideals of beauty, decency, and truth. In *The Rise of Silas Lapham,* Howells tests and illustrates his theory partly through the love plot, which sets up precisely the situation of *Tears, Idle Tears.*

Irene Lapham, beautiful but culturally limited, falls in love with the patrician Tom Corey. Everyone assumes Corey is interested in Irene, whereas he has fallen in love with the older sister, Penelope. Penelope has a lively wit, a gift for mimicry, and an independent way of seeing and storytelling. She is described as "dark," not because she is sultry but because in contrast to her sister's lovely color she is not beautiful. At first Penelope epitomizes the realistic novelist, sensible, acute at social observation, and intelligent about character and values. But the sentimental ethos of self-sacrifice retains considerable power; it infiltrates the consciousness of a character as sensible as the appropriately named Penelope. She succumbs, decides it would be wrong to accept Corey, but finally comes to her senses, marries him, and vindicates Howells's version of realism. Irene does, too. She suffers, matures, and, instead of either pining away or marrying, remains single, with the author's full approval.

MIDDLE-CLASS WOMEN IN *SILAS LAPHAM*

But however much Howells seems assured in his view that finally everyone agrees on what is true and lifelike, in practice he recognizes important strains and qualifications. It is significant that the women in the novel collaborate in constructing the conventional love story of the beautiful but limited Irene and the handsome patrician, Tom Corey, as if Corey could not be interested in the lively realist, Penelope, the "dark," unglamorous one. By exposing their susceptibility to a false, sentimental way of seeing, Howells is illuminating an important crack in the edifice of the middle-class true woman, since in this ideology women are the guardians of moral value and conscience. Mrs. Lapham plays a central role in misperceiving and constructing the love story. Howells is particularly astute in showing that Mrs. Lapham has suffered a serious decline. In the early days of her marriage she was actively involved in Lapham's affairs, but as they become more prosperous she loses touch. She simultaneously sees less clearly than she did in the early, hard working years.

Displaced from the world of affairs, Mrs. Lapham at one point becomes insanely jealous of the attractive "typewriter" or secretary who is at home in Lapham's office. Mrs. Lapham's hysteria is driven by her sense that she no longer has a useful economic function. Instead, her main function in life is to be a moral guide and her confidence in her judgment has been seriously weakened. For Howells the situation of prosperous middle-class women is both enviable and precarious. In *A Hazard of New Fortunes* (1890), it becomes even more extreme. Mrs. Dryfoos, Mrs. Lapham's successor, is separated by her husband's wealth from her original rural home and religious tradition. She is an invalid with no connection to the confusing urban world her children must negotiate. Howells shows that the old republican virtues of simplicity, hard work, and suspicion of luxury are not easy to sustain in the new America of stock gambling, capital expansion, and the self-made millionaire. Howells is particularly sensitive to the dilemmas of prosperity for women caught in the crosscurrents of republicanism and capitalism or in the conflicts internal to the republican tradition.

MONEY AND GUILT

In *The Rise of Silas Lapham,* Mrs. Lapham contributes to the dilemmas centering on money, business, and success. At the outset of Lapham's career, Mrs. Lapham is the one who realizes that to convert Lapham's paint mine into a gold mine, capital is required. She persuades him to take a partner, Rogers, to supply the capital necessary for full development and expansion. Partly because Rogers is not competent, partly because Lapham wants sole control of what he worships, the paint, Lapham forces Rogers out of the business. He does it legally, fairly, and precisely as any reasonable capitalist would but Mrs. Lapham's conscience is troubled because Lapham has taken advantage of Rogers in favor of his own self-interest. A kind of original sin is involved, since Lapham's prosperity is inseparable from his use of Rogers's capital. Rogers and his capital plus Lapham's hard work and good judgment lead to growth, wealth, and the ambiguous morality connected with ambition and big money.

The ambiguity is grounded in the agrarian, republican values that animate Mrs. Lapham's conscience. The paint in its original condition is associated with the old rural, republican world: it is rooted in the land itself, vividly symbolized by the ore clinging to the exposed roots of a great tree. The paint comes from the old farm, associated with Lapham's father and the graves of the family. Once Mrs. Lapham introduces Rogers and his capital, financial success follows but the earlier virtues are tainted. Mrs. Lapham cannot accept that to succeed as a capitalist, Lapham must behave impersonally. Her conscience keeps alive what she sees as the wrong Lapham committed. In this paradigm of the move from the old republican, agrarian America to the new America of large fortunes and capital expansion, Howells taps into conflicts deeply encoded in the republican's relation to capitalism. For Howells, Mrs. Lapham's conscience is both a strength and a nagging, punitive weakness.

THE DISEASED BUSINESSMAN

As for Lapham, his wife accuses him of making the paint his God and worshiping it. Under the pressure of Rogers's capital and the dynamics of capitalistic growth, the worship of paint begins to merge with the worship of money as God. Howells handles this change circumspectly, not overtly, in that Lapham continues to value primarily the tangible, earth-grounded product. But Lapham knows that "you wouldn't want my life without my money," and when he is with the patrician Coreys he brags incessantly about his money as well as his paint. Under his no-nonsense surface, Lapham has also been infected with the virus of social ambition, not so much for himself as for his daughters. He has bought a prize piece of property on the Back Bay and he decides to build an impressive house so that his family can be in society.

All of Lapham's underlying social longings and feelings about money and class difference come to a focus in the house. At the outset Mrs. Lapham also connects the house and all it stands for with Rogers and with Lapham's success. "You can sell it for all me," Mrs. Lapham says. "I shan't live in it. There's blood on it."

Lapham may not worship money but he does worship the house. The house is the beautiful embodiment of the new self as distinct from the old Jeffersonian, republican self of Lapham's origins. The republicans had a deep suspicion of luxury and of wealth gained through financial speculation. Lapham is infatuated with the lovely, luxurious improvements his architect suggests. Lapham also finances the house partly from money he has recently made as a stock gambler. Republicans, moreover, valued a general equality of conditions, not the economic, social, and class differences the house symbolizes. In Howells's recognizable version, republicans stress restraint, self-control, discipline, moderation, and a life lived close to the land, symbolically in the old house on the patriarchal farm.

To satisfy his wife and perhaps his own sense of right and wrong, Lapham lends Rogers money and accepts stock in return. To save his original investment, Lapham becomes more deeply entangled with Rogers, he gambles on the market, and he suffers serious losses. The market for paint is glutted and a competitor has a product that undersells Lapham's. At a key moment in this gradually developing scenario, Lapham realizes that to save his business he must sell the unfinished house. Although his pride is deeply wounded, he decides to go ahead. But instead he accidentally burns the house to the ground. The usually careful Lapham, moreover, has neglected to renew the insurance, so that the house is a total loss.

SILAS'S MORAL RISE

The result is that Lapham begins to purge or expiate the wrongs of a violated republicanism through what amounts to a valued act of self-sacrifice, a sacrifice of the possession that embodies the new self Lapham has achieved as a self-made man. Lapham's self-sacrifice contrasts and develops in counterpoint with Penelope's *Tears, Idle Tears* version. Also in contrast to *Tears, Idle Tears* and in accord with his own views about realism, Howells does not have Lapham make a conscious decision to behave virtuously and heroically. Instead, Howells has a sure sense of unconscious motivation rooted in the morally charged conflicts of a possessive market society and the American republican tradition.

In the sequel, Lapham, a secular Job or Christ, faces up to a series of temptations Rogers poses.[1] Lapham consciously chooses to sacrifice his own self-interest—his business and fortune—rather than to take advantage of a legal but morally shady scheme to defraud a group of idealistic English investors. As the Satan-figure in this drama, Rogers is a plausibly rendered businessman who manipulates his appear-

---

1. Like Christ's, Job's faith was tested by both suffering and temptation.

ance of "bland and beneficent caution," just as he turns to his own advantage his republican surface as "a man of just, sober, and prudent views, fixed purposes, and the good citizenship that avoids debt and hazard of every kind." His arguments are as specious and plausible as his appearance. Lapham and the reader, however, easily see through the mask. In this important respect Howells contrasts with those contemporaries, predecessors, and successors for whom the deceptions and acquisitive impulses make for irreducible epistemological uncertainty.

At the end Howells arranges it so that Lapham returns to his origins on the patriarchal, republican farm. He moves back into the old home and runs a scaled-down version of his business. He regains both the good sense and the moral virtue he lost under Rogers's influence. His fall in fortune corresponds with a rise in virtue. In illustrating the success of failure, Lapham thus validates Howells's belief in the agrarian, republican tradition. Lapham also exposes a weakness in Howells's theory of realism, since the pastoral ending highlights the contrast between Howells's deepest values and the underlying realities of an increasingly urban, industrialized market society. The metaphysical and empirical sides of Howells's theory do not really coincide in the emerging America of the 1880s and 1890s.

THE COMPLEXITY OF HOWELLS AND JAMES

Far from being literal and artless, Howells's practice of realism is full of revealing contradictions, nuances, and a suggestive interplay between surface and depth. The same holds for the other realists of the post–Civil War era, although the precise content and intensity vary from writer to writer and novel to novel. Art and imagination, moreover, are central concerns of the American realists. Cumulatively, they give us a complex sense of the fate of the imagination and its creations in the context of a vital, changing America. . . . Sometimes sensitive to the moral and ideological conflicts, as in Howells, sometimes to the moral, epistemological, and sociopolitical implications, as in James, American realists explored the intimate connection between houses and selves, between possessions and character in the new America. They were also unusually alert to the situation of women, as in . . . Howells's insights into the consequences of prosperity, and James's awareness of Isabel's fear and freedom.

Money in all its implications is the other major preoccupation of nineteenth- and twentieth-century realism. On this count the post–Civil War American writers are as full and perceptive as we can ask for. Their sense of reality is open and varied, responsive to the surfaces and recesses of American selves and society.

Realism and the African-American Novel

William L. Andrews

Realism and its literary variations were an attempt to absorb, reflect, and engage the social and political events that swept through America between the Civil War and World War I. William Andrews illustrates the extent to which three classic African-American novels of this era adopted the techniques of Realism and Naturalism to voice African Americans' place in post–Civil War America. With the abandonment of Reconstruction in 1877, an "Age of Reaction" set in. Reactionary state legislatures in the South sought to once again impose white supremacy and thwart any social and political aspirations on the part of African Americans. Frances Harper asserted the power of African-American womanhood and need for racial uplift. Charles Chesnutt used Realism as a weapon to expose and protest racial hatred and the violence it engendered. Paul Laurence Dunbar adopted the Naturalist techniques of Crane, Dreiser and Norris to explore a new social phenomenon of the 1890s: the movement of a significant number of African Americans away from the South, as they pursued the dream of jobs and equality in the urban centers of the North. William L. Andrews teaches American and African-American Literature at the University of North Carolina. He is the author of *To Tell a Free Story: the First Century of Afro-American Autobiography, 1760–1865* (1986), and *The Literary Career of Charles Chesnutt* (1980).

By bringing Reconstruction to an end in the South in 1877, the Republican party in the North and its partners in big business and finance served notice of their willingness to

Excerpted from *The African-American Novel in the Age of Reaction: Three Classics,* by William L. Andrews (New York: Mentor, 1992). Reprinted with permission from the author.

bargain away black civil rights in the South in exchange for a white-controlled political system receptive to northern investment. Many white supremacists found federal encouragement in the 1883 U.S. Supreme Court ruling that declared the most far-reaching civil rights legislation passed during Reconstruction to be unconstitutional. During the late 1880s the first laws mandating segregation in railroad transportation swept through the South. The 1890s saw first Mississippi, then South Carolina, and eventually every southern state systematically altering its constitution to deny blacks the right to vote. When the Supreme Court ruled in 1896 in favor of the South's "separate but equal" racial doctrine, the federal government put its stamp of approval on state laws requiring cradle-to-grave segregation of the races. An age of reaction, which threatened to reverse all the political and economic advances black America had earned since Emancipation, settled over the United States. Realizing that they could no longer expect support from the federal government in their struggle for dignity and opportunity in the South, many blacks concluded that their best hope lay in cultivating their own resources for the uplifting of the race. Among these resources was the literary imagination, which writers like Frances Ellen Watkins Harper believed could be used both to inspire blacks to high ideals and to educate whites about the capacities and achievements of African-Americans.

FRANCES HARPER AND RACIAL UPLIFT

In *Iola Leroy* (1892), the culminating work of Harper's remarkable literary career, a major character issues a call for the kind of African-American writing to which Harper devoted herself throughout her adult life: "out of the race must come its own defenders. With them [i.e., black Americans] the pen must be mightier than the sword. It is the weapon of civilization, and they must use it in their own defense.". . .

The novel begins at a moment late in the Civil War when a group of North Carolina slaves realize they have the opportunity to escape bondage and join the approaching Union army. Some of the slaves make plans immediately to seize their freedom, while others resolve to remain at home, some because of obligations to family members, and in one instance because of a sense of loyalty to a master. Notable here is Harper's emphasis on the diversity of the slaves' sense of purpose and responsibility. Immediate personal freedom is all-in-all to some, but just as understandable and respectable are those who set aside their individual desires and choose instead to honor previous commitments to others. This tension between personal fulfillment and identification with the welfare of the group—be it the black family, the black community, or humanity in general—is debated repeatedly in *Iola Leroy* and is resolved by every major character in the same way, that is, by placing the best interests of others before self-satisfaction.

This theme of altruistic self-sacrifice is just one way in which *Iola Leroy* displays its ties to the nineteenth-century tradition of women's fiction. The title character of the novel confronts challenges to her moral and social ideals reminiscent of those that the heroines of popular white women's fiction had to contend with. These challenges are epitomized in Iola's decision, not once but twice in the novel, to reject the marriage proposal of a sincere white suitor, Dr. Gresham. Again, however, Harper's adoption of the conventions of a well-established type of fiction bears her distinctive stamp. For when Iola Leroy ponders the ultimate decision a woman must make in nineteenth-century fiction, that is, whether and whom to marry, Iola does so as an *African-American* woman. Every choice she makes as a typical women's fiction heroine—how to recover her long-lost mother, how to support herself, whom to reject and accept in marriage—she considers in light of the fact that she has chosen to identify herself as a black person. To Harper such an identification amounts to an almost holy calling of service to the least advantage of black Americans. If Iola Leroy seems at times so wise and noble and self-sacrificial as to be a virtually bloodless ideal, one should remember that until Harper's novel no African-American female character had been treated as worthy of such idealization in the nineteenth-century women's fiction tradition. Basing her heroine's moral superiority on her dedication to the welfare of black people rather than on her superficial affinities with whites was Harper's way of arguing that even the most talented and privileged of black women had to conceive of their traditional responsibilities to family as embracing the entire black community. Thus even when Iola decides to marry, it is with the understanding that she and her African-American husband will return to the South to "labor for those who had passed form the old oligarchy of slavery into the new commonwealth of freedom."

Set in the turbulent years of the Civil War and early Reconstruction, *Iola Leroy* deplores southern mob violence, including public lynchings and other atrocities, and condemns efforts in the South to deprive the freedpeople of the right to vote. In keeping with the antislavery movement's belief that society would reform only when the hearts of its individual members were redeemed, Harper appealed to the conscience of her readers as the ultimate wellspring of social change. . . .

CHARLES CHESNUTT AND RACISM IN POST–CIVIL WAR AMERICA

At the end of Charles W. Chesnutt's *The Marrow of Tradition* (1901), the leading male character, who is, like Harper's Dr. Latimer, a light-skinned black physician laboring in the South for the welfare of his people, has much less reason to contemplate his region's future hopefully. The town of Wellington, North Carolina, where Chesnutt's novel is set, has just undergone a terrible race riot, plotted and directed by a cadre of white supremacists intent on overturning the town's biracial, democratically elected government. Few who read *The Marrow of Tradition* when it first appeared would have overlooked the similarity of the novel's climactic events to the infamous Wilmington Massacre of November 1898, when violent means were used to impose white supremacy on a North Carolina town that Chesnutt had often visited during his youth. Although born in Cleveland, Ohio, in 1858, Charles Waddell Chesnutt grew up in Fayetteville, North Carolina, scarcely one hundred miles up the Cape Fear River from Wilmington. . . .

REALISM AS A WEAPON

His first literary success came in August 1887, when the *Atlantic Monthly* published "The Goophered Grapevine," an unusual dialect story that featured Chesnutt's knowledge of southern black "hoodoo" practices as well as his subtle, ironic wit. For the next decade Chesnutt worked at the craft of short-story writing. He was eventually rewarded in 1899 with the publication of two collections of his stories, *The Conjure Woman*, composed of a series of tales of slave life patterned after "The Goophered Grapevine," and *The Wife of His Youth and Other Stories of the Color Line*, a volume concerned primarily with the problems faced by people like Chesnutt, that is, light-skinned, middle-class African-Americans who lived in the urban North. Houghton Mifflin, Chesnutt's prestigious Boston publisher, was sufficiently pleased by the sales of his short story collections and by the positive reviews written by such eminent literary figures as William Dean Howells that it wasted little time in bringing out Chesnutt's first novel, *The House Behind the Cedars,* in 1900. This book about a beautiful young woman who attempts to pass for white helped intro-duce Chesnutt as a social problem novelist. He hoped his sec-ond and more hard-hitting novel of purpose, *The Marrow of Tradition,* would cement his grasp on a large readership and have the kind of impact on public opinion that *Uncle Tom's Cabin* had had fifty years earlier. Unfortunately, although *The Marrow of Tradition* was widely reviewed as timely and provocative, it did not sell well enough to satisfy its author. Chesnutt would publish one more novel about racial condi-tions in the South, *The Colonel's Dream* (1905), but after the disappointing reception of *The Marrow of Tradition,* he treated fiction writing as an avocation rather than a full-time career. Through the early decades of the twentieth century, black American held his turn-of-the-century fiction in high esteem because of its literary craftsmanship, realistic treat-ment of the American color line, and commitment to racial justice. Today Chesnutt is generally recognized as the first African-American novelist to engage a substantial national audience with a seriously conceived and artistically sophisti-cated social message. . . .

A CLASSIC OF AMERICAN REALISM

The Marrow of Tradition's main thread of action knits to-gether the lives of two families: the Carterets, who represent the postwar southern aristocracy, and the Millers, a mixed-race couple who embody their creator's idea of the progres-sive New Negro. Philip Carteret's obsession with white su-premacy leads him to mastermind the race riot that destroys Dr. Miller's hospital in the process of overthrowing Welling-ton's government. Carteret's wife, Olivia, also poisoned by racism and envy, has long disavowed her relationship to her half-sister, Janet Miller, wife of the black doctor and the product of a secret marriage between a white aristocrat and his former slave. In spite of each Carteret's best efforts to keep separate from the Millers and to maintain their supposed superiority over them, fate repeatedly implicates each family in the fortunes of the other. At the end of the novel Philip Carteret is forced to acknowledge his dependence on Dr. Miller for the medical skill that can save Carteret's mortally ill son. Olivia Carteret is also forced to acknowledge Janet Miller as her legitimate half-sister and rightful co-heir to their father's estate. Chesnutt thus managers the outcome of *The Marrow of Tradition* so as to remind his readers that artificial caste and class divisions cannot permanently sever the ties that bind humanity together in mutual social need and moral obligation.

Just as *Iola Leroy* represents a notable African-American contribution to antislavery and women's fiction traditions, so *The Marrow of Tradition* displays clear affiliations with the late nineteenth-century school of American realism. Unlike the idealized mulattas and mulattos of Harper's imagination, William and Janet Miller are conceived with distinct strengths and weaknesses. Their personal desires and self-interest sometimes vie with their perception of what Harper would have regarded as their higher mission. The Millers' internal struggles, which would seem out of place in *Iola Leroy*, reveal Chesnutt's commitment to represent honestly the ambivalences that he felt characterized the situation of many mixed-race people. William Miller's foil in the novel, Josh Green , a working-class black man willing to die to defend his people, might be regarded as more heroic than the circumspect mixed-race physician who refuses to sacrifice himself to the cause of violent resistance to Carteret's henchmen. Yet in the almost Darwinian world of *The Marrow of Tradition*, it is Miller, not Green, who survives the bloody massacre and is then able to take a difficult step toward healing the wounds exacerbated by the new white racism. Consistent with the perspective of such realist writers as William Dean Howells and Edith Wharton, Chesnutt remained convinced that, despite the heavy weight of tradition oppressing the ascendant forces of change in the South, individual moral initiative could still make a positive difference. The closing line of *The Marrow of Tradition*—"there's time enough, but none to spare"—testifies to Chesnutt's determination to be realistic about the precariousness of the southern situation without sounding so pessimistic about its solution that his readers would decide the region's racial problems were hopeless.

THE AFRICAN-AMERICAN "POET LAUREATE"

The final bleak lines of Paul Laurence Dunbar's *The Sport of the Gods* (1902)—"they knew they were powerless against some Will infinitely stronger than their own"—stands in stark contrast to both the assured optimism of *Iola Leroy's* conclusion and the urgent call for action implicit in the ending of *The Marrow of Tradition.* Yet if there was one black writer at the turn of the century whom most American readers would not have considered despairing, especially about black people's lot in life, it would have been Paul Laurence Dunbar. Dubbed the "Poet Laureate of the Negro race" by Booker T. Washington, Dunbar was best known for his lively verse in black dialect, which earned the praise of sophisticated critics and popular readers alike. But he also produced a sizable body of short stories and novels, of which *The Sport of the Gods* has received considerable attention as a major novel of protest and the first extensive portrayal in fiction of life in twentieth-century Harlem. . . .

During a triumphal reading tour in Great Britain in 1897 Dunbar went to work on his first novel, *The Uncalled* (1898), which, though a competently-told (and somewhat autobiographical) story of a young man who refuses to enter the ministry, was coolly reviewed because of its lack of African-American local color. Simultaneous with his first novel, Dunbar also brought out his first collection of short stories, *Folks from Dixie,* which dealt with black people from both the slavery era and the post-Reconstruction period. Many of the stories in this and three subsequent volumes of Dunbar's short fiction celebrate the simple pleasures of "down home" living for black Americans, who find fulfillment in their own communities apart from and seemingly unmindful of the world of whites. Only a comparative few of Dunbar's stories offer candid assessments of social problems occasioned by race. Typically the difficulties that blacks face in his stories arise from their own self-deceptions and misplaced priorities, not from deeper causes, such as white racism, that would require a profounder analysis of social and economic forces. Occasionally, however, Dunbar put aside the mask of sentiment, piety, and easy moralizing that he generally wore for the readers of his fiction, revealing his doubts about the faith in self-help maintained by a Frances Harper or the hope for social reform that a Charles Chesnutt clung to. *The Sport of the Gods* represents Dunbar's most thoroughgoing critique of myths that he, as well as Harper and Chesnutt, had subscribed to in much of their fiction, particularly the myth of the southern black community as self-sustaining and ultimately triumphant over injustice through a combination of faith in God and commitment to social struggle. As a foray into a grim, urban realism anticipating the work of Richard Wright, *The Sport of the Gods* might have signaled a turning point in the artistic evolution of Paul Laurence Dunbar. Unfortunately, the author's worsening health and harried finances allowed him little time or energy to explore this literary vein before his death in 1906.

DUNBAR'S NOVEL OF THE CITY

Just as *Iola Leroy* and *The Marrow of Tradition* are grounded in crucial historical developments and social issues of the post-Reconstruction years and the white supremacists 1890s, respectively, so *The Sport of the Gods* addresses a major question affecting black America at the turn of the century—the advantages and disadvantages of black migration from the rural South to the urban North. As early as 1879 African-Americans had begun to leave the South in search of better opportunities on the plains of the Midwest. But not until the turn of the century did significantly large numbers of black southerners set their sights on northeastern big cities, launching what has come to be known as the "great migrations" of the first decades of the twentieth century. For Dunbar *The Sport of the Gods* serves as a kind of case study of migration, and he leaves little room in his chronicle of frustration and demoralization for anything but a negative judgment of the fate of black families who try to resettle in a city like New York. Explaining the causes of the tragedy of the Hamilton family in Harlem, Dunbar does not cite such familiar aspects of de facto racism in the North as joblessness or poor housing or restricted educational opportunity for blacks. Instead the author illustrates the lack of real community in northern cities, the empty hedonism, the collapse of "home life," and the indifference to the "old traditions" and "old teachings" that had long sustained black Americans, particularly in the South. Dunbar suggests that this lack of a moral and cultural foundation for a viable black community in the northern city almost guarantees that a well-meaning mother like Fannie Hamilton will fail to protect her children from exploitation by the hustlers and hangers-on who make up "the fast life" in Harlem. Revealing the futility of individual human will against destructive social forces unleashed in the city, *The Sport of the Gods* takes a leaf from novels of urban naturalism such as Stephen Crane's *Maggie: A Girl of the Streets* (1893) and Theodore Dreiser's *Sister Carrie* (1900).

DUNBAR'S REJECTION OF "HARD LINE NATURALISM"

After reading *The Sport of the Gods*, however, one comes away with the feeling that Dunbar found little consolation in the themes of human futility and fatalism that arise from his portrayal of black migration. Unwilling or unable to assume the posture of nonjudgmental detachment favored by the naturalist, Dunbar betrays a lingering allegiance to the moral idealism and activism of Harper and Chesnutt, even as he portrays their standards as quaintly alien to the code of the Harlemites who serve as the agents of the Hamilton family's dissolution. This desire for an alternative to mere cynicism helps explain the strongly satirical tone that the novelist takes toward many of his characters, including whites and blacks in the South and the North, conservative and "liberal" alike. Yet *The Sport of the Gods* lacks the moral consistency of great satire; even its attitude toward the city itself fluctuates between outrage and admiration, disgust and gusto. In other words *The Sport of the Gods*, much more than *Iola Leroy* or *The Marrow of Tradition*, is caught up in, and is indeed the expression of, a vision of irreconcilable contradictions in African-American life. At the end of the story Dunbar gives Berry and Fannie Hamilton a final respite from some of the more oppressive of these contradictions, but even this apparent sop to the weary reader cannot disguise the structural irony of the novel. After all, what does it mean that at the start of the story a hypocritical white self-protectiveness banishes the Hamiltons from their home, while at the end an equally contemptible white self-aggrandizement restores them to it? Is one supposed to feel relieved or dispirited, happy or sad, by this double reversal of the Hamiltons' fortunes at the hands of white "gods" who become themselves the sport of the author's irony? . . .

THE FATE OF THE BLACK FAMILY

The fate of the black family in *Iola Leroy, The Marrow of Tradition,* and *The Sport of the Gods* serves as an index to the differences among Harper, Chesnutt, and Dunbar with regard to their novels' social vision and aesthetic credo. Harper's is a novel of unabashed family reunion. Its firmly resolved plot may be read as a metaphor of her belief that the African-American struggle could be brought to a just and meaningful conclusion and that art could and should serve as a light of inspiration toward that end. Chesnutt's tempered and chastened realism compelled him to balance one family's loss with another family's potential restoration at the conclusion of *The Marrow of Tradition*. By revealing the tragedy suffered by a black family because of white malice and indifference, Chesnutt hoped to drive home the necessity of his readers' taking the reins of his open-ended plot so as to bring the nation's story to resolution in a just social union. Dunbar's emphasis on the dissolution of a black family and its irretrievable loss testifies ostensibly to his inability to envision a community for blacks in northern cities or an alternative to their traditional roles as dependents on whites in the rural South. Yet the fact that Dunbar, of all turn-of-the-century African-American writers, determined to sing his urban blues without offering a shadow of a solution beyond the singing itself is perhaps more significant to the future of African-American literature than the work of Harper or Chesnutt. For in the unresolved, and seemingly unresolvable, problems that Dunbar posed in *The Sport of the Gods* we find the incipient call for a new fiction to confront new phenomena—the northern urban ghetto and the consciousness it instilled in black people—in ways that would take African-American fiction beyond the moral categories and accepted literary modes of the nineteenth century and place it in the forefront of the modern American novel.

Women Writers and Women Characters in American Realism

Cecelia Tichi

The final three decades of the nineteenth century
saw the beginnings of a change in the image and
role of women in American life. A significant number of female authors published novels and short
stories in the 1890's and early 1900's. Writers such as
Kate Chopin, Sarah Orne Jewett, Mary Wilkins Freeman, Ellen Glasgow, and Willa Cather came from
different regions of the country and have often been
characterized as "regional" or "local color" writers.
However, all of them confronted in one way or another themes impacting women, such as marriage,
sexual freedom, individual identity, and the female
subconscious. Cecelia Tichi is a Professor of American Literature and American Studies at Vanderbilt
University. Her publications include *New World, New
Earth: Environmental Reform in American Literature
from the Puritans through Whitman* (1979) and *Shifting Gears: Technology, Literature, Culture in Modern
America* (1987).

"Molly Donahue have up an' become a new woman!" So begins [journalist] Finley Peter Dunne's satirical "Mr. Dooley"
sketch "On the New Woman" (1898), in which the Irish Molly
has sorely tested her husband by riding a bicycle, demanding
to vote, and "wearin' clothes that no lady shud wear." Now
Molly proclaims "she'll be no man's slave." Henceforth a
woman like her will "wear what clothes she wants [and] earn
her own livin'," no longer to be given over in marriage to a
"clown" who makes her "dipindant" on male whims.

Mr. Dooley's sketch, which pivots on the reversal of traditional male-female roles, ends in Molly's capitulation to her

husband and a reassertion of the status quo in which women will "stay at home an' dredge in th' house wurruk." But if Molly is mollified for the price of a new shawl, her cause is not so easily set aside. When Mr. Dooley spoofed the new woman of the 1890s, he affirmed her importance. The Chicago-based Dunne, America's foremost political-social satirist, acknowledged the status of "the New Woman" when he gave her equal space with such topics as American imperialism in the Philippines, military adventurism in Cuba, Populist politics, and the Dreyfus case.[1]

In fact, the new woman demanded attention because, as Dunne recognized, she was a powerful social-literary figure by the late nineteenth century. She both embodied new values and posed a critical challenge to the existing order. And she affected the national literature. From the 1890s the new woman—independent, outspoken, iconoclastic—empowered the work of Kate Chopin, Alice James, Charlotte Perkins Gilman, Edith Wharton, Ellen Glasgow, Willa Cather, and the young Gertrude Stein, even if Wharton denounced "the new theories . . . that awful women rave about on platforms." The new woman, moreover, was incumbent in American literature in the previous decades. Wharton disparaged the "rose-and-lavender" pages of Sarah Orne Jewett and Mary E. Wilkins Freeman, but the idea of the new woman occupies an incipient, covert place in their careers and writings, which have subversive thematic implications.

In literature and social history the new woman comes to mind most readily in the familiar image of the 1920s Jazz Age flapper with the bobbed hair and boyish figure that proclaimed the personal freedom foreclosed to her grandmother. The new woman, however, had a decades-long developmental background. By the 1890s she was an important part of the era's flouting of middle-class convention. Women on both sides of the Atlantic were challenging the foundations of a patriarchal society.

It is fair to say that from the 1880s the new woman in theory and fact changed the canon of American literature, affecting writers' lives and invigorating the national literature with new fictional design in character, form, and theme. At a period when the men's *Bildungsroman*,[2] was urban and in-

---

1. The Dreyfus Case exposed corruption and anti-semitism in 1890's France. 2. a kind of novel that typically maps the character-building struggles and ultimate triumph of an individual's journey through life

dustrial; and based upon such scientific "laws" as Darwinism, the ethos of the new woman engendered a fiction of what must be called women's regionality. It sought to establish alternative bases of consciousness and to show how consciousness itself could be deployed for women's empowerment. Its design was iconoclastic, challenging the very premises on which men's fictional worlds were constructed.

Alice James, for instance, challenged the presumptions of a patriarchal culture in her diary and her letters spanning the period from the 1880s until her death in 1892. James offers a running commentary on various male physicians baffled by the symptoms from which she suffered for most of her adult life. James's doctors, representatives in her mind of social authority and expertise, prove to be vapid and mechanical. As a patient, James learned that these male authorities, "all terrible," presented "a spectacle of paralysis . . . talking by the hour without *saying* anything."

REGIONALISM AND THE THEME OF MARRIAGE

James's contemporaries were also challenging the received wisdom on courtship, marriage, and the family, rejecting such "truths" as the maternal instinct and the role of child-rearing as the highest duty of women. One of Sarah Orne Jewett's characters in *A Country Doctor* (1884) remarks acidly that it "cannot be the proper vocation of all women to bring up children, so many of them are dead failures at it." And in *The Awakening* (1899), Kate Chopin, a widow and mother of six, brought biographical experience to bear when she presented a character who disparaged "marriages which masquerade as the decrees of Fate," and satirized the "women who idolized their children, worshipped their husbands, and esteemed it a holy privilege to efface themselves as individuals and grow wings as ministering angels." Like-minded feminists proposed that women's health would improve if sports and rational dress replaced the whalebone of the conventional middle-class woman, a point that Gilman argued in her fiction of the 1910s.

The new woman proposed to seek personal fulfillment through work instead of matrimony. In *A Country Doctor*, Sarah Jewett's young female protagonist wishes "she had been trained as boys are, to the work of their lives!," then feels like "a reformer, a radical, and even like a political agitator" as she decides to forgo housekeeping and enter a profession. Rhetorically she asks, "Would you have me bury the talent God his given me?" Jewett was not alone. In *Virginia* (1913), Ellen Glasgow wrote sarcastically of the Southern woman bred for genteel idleness even in the era of the post-bellum industrial South. How humiliating, she says wryly, for a mother "to train her daughter in any profitable occupation which might have lifted her out of the class of unskilled labour in which indigent gentlewomen by right belonged." Through their own commitment to professional writing, figures like Glasgow, Jewett, and others were able to understand, and to propound, the importance of self-fulfilling work outside the sphere of domesticity.

SEXUAL FREEDOM AND IDENTITY

Central to literary portrayals of the new woman was the idea of women's sexual freedom, including the right to abstain and to choose sexual partners in or out of marital relationships. By the 1910s, when Margaret Sanger had opened her birth-control clinic in New York City, journalists proclaimed "sex o'clock in America." Certain literary texts, meanwhile, had argued that sexual freedom was a woman's prerogative. Such was the erotic life Chopin chronicled in her (posthumously published) story of a married woman's afternoon affair with a former suitor: "Her firm, elastic flesh . . . was knowing for the first time its birthright" ("The Storm"). A woman's extramarital sexual pleasure, Chopin suggests, can coexist with a satisfying domestic life.

From the 1890s, then, the new woman had a recognizable identity, one derived largely from the rational, analytical demystification of the "fair sex." Like Mr. Dooley's Molly, the new woman could resolve to earn her own living, as did Freeman, Gilman, and Cather, and, like Glasgow and Stein, be confident of personal fulfillment outside the marital or familial relationship, which she viewed as a form of slavery. Ellen Glasgow remarks on this point. Her Virginia Pendleton "let her mother slave over her because she had been born into a world where the slaving of mothers was a part of the natural order, and she had not as yet become independent enough to question the morality of the commonplace."

As Glasgow's statement indicates, the idea of conscious choice in and of itself was a hallmark of the identity of the new woman, who was very much a middle-class figure, since women lower on the socioeconomic ladder, laborers for decades as domestics and as factory operatives, were not at liberty to shape their lives according to such principles. For the privileged new woman, however, the principles were paramount. Her modernity was neither whimsical nor idiosyncratic, but based upon intellectually informed (and personally distressing) analyses of woman's place in contemporary society. Kate Chopin's character from *The Awakening*, Edna Pontellier, an upper middle-class wife and mother, determines to have her "own way," knowing "that is wanting a great deal . . . when you have to trample upon the lives, the hearts, the prejudices of others." Early in life Edna understands the duality of the "outward existence which conforms, the inward life which questions." But the new woman was not content to continue the duality nor to sustain its terms of conformity and concealment. Because her priority, like Edna's, was in large part sexual, the new woman posed serious challenge to the status quo, for she could not be dismissed as a prostitute or a fallen woman. Her radicalism was a matter of personal deci sion. It did not take the form of an organized political movement. No congresses or conventions mark its history. In this sense it was individualistic, operating in the spheres open to personal choice, from sexual preference to dress.

Sketched in this light, the new woman can seem a model of enablement for aspirant women writers like Chopin, Gilman, Cather, Wharton, Glasgow, and others, all of them middle-class figures (with the exception of the upper-class Wharton) who ranged in age from their twenties to their forties when Mr. Dooley's "New Woman" appeared in American newspapers. For these writers, additionally, the new woman pertained directly to the matter of literary succession. Their female predecessors in nineteenth-century American literature, best-selling authors like Louisa May Alcott, Susan Warner, and Harriet Beecher Stowe, had prospered with fiction only covertly insurrectionist, fiction congenial to an era that idealized the values of the virtuous, home-loving woman in her proper domestic sphere. In hindsight it seems inevitable that this new generation of American women writers would undertake revisionist fiction formulating the viewpoint of the new woman. . . .

THE COST OF WRITING THE "TRUTH"

Of course the new woman's writing criticized and defied traditional values, but the fate of Kate Chopin speaks volumes about the cultural retribution on the woman writer whose literary treatment of her subject offended convention by daring to give readers "the unaccustomed taste of candor." Reaching her full powers in *The Awakening,* a novel explicitly concerned with women's sexual passions, Chopin was devastated by the audience rejection, which took the form of hostile reviews, librarians' refusal to circulate her novel in her native city of St. Louis, and the snubbing by that city's Fine Arts Club, which declined to make her a member. Friends shunned her as reviewers called *The Awakening* morbid, poisonous, and vulgar. One friend said Chopin was "crushed," and she wrote very little in the remaining five years of her life. She felt "left by the wayside" as she herself wrote in a short sketch—"struck mute" as [critic] Larzer Ziff has so accurately written.

WOMEN'S REGIONALISM

Thus the new-woman writers walked a narrow line between frankness and the ostracism that frankness might incur. They rejected the camouflage of domesticity but gained acceptance, many of them, under another rubric—regionalism. Until recently, which is to say until feminist critics began reevaluation of their work, Jewett and Freeman, together with Chopin, Glasgow, and Cather, were considered to be regionalists or even local colorists, writers faithful to particular geographical areas whose cultural patterns of speech, manners, and habits they accurately reflect, often in tones of affectionate nostalgia. In this light Jewett and Freeman become memorialists of a faded New England, Glasgow of the Virginian South, Cather of the pioneers' Nebraska where she grew up, and Chopin of French Creole Louisiana. Wharton, metaphorically a regionalist of the terrain of High Society, also brought the dark naturalist's focus to bear upon New England in *Ethan Frome* (1911) and *Summer* (1917).

The regionalist label was in part justified. Jewett vivified the world of rural Maine, while Freeman's collections, such as *A Humble Romance* (1887) and *A New England Nun* (1891), feature the artifacts of a New England fast disappearing in metropolitan America: calico, patchwork quilts, braided rugs, the garden patch, the domestic memorabilia of "brown loaves and flaky pies—the proofs of . . . love and culinary skill." So in Glasgow we find Virginian honeysuckle, cornmeal "soap," loyal darkies, mint juleps, fox hunts, while Chopin's fiction abounds with the accoutrements of French-Creole Louisiana, where women sip wine and spirits, smoke cigarettes, and enjoy men's risqué stories. Chopin's *Bayou Folk* (1894) and Cather's *O Pioneers!* (1913) indicate the regional appeal to readers leading increasingly urbanized lives in a metropolitan America looking nostalgically upon its past. Under cover of regionalism, however, these women writers explored the territory of women's lives. Their essential agenda in the era of the new woman was to map the geography of their gender. They were regionalists—but not solely in the ways critics have conventionally thought. The geography of America formed an important part of their work, but essentially they charted the regions of women's lives, regions both without and within the self.

THE INNER REGIONS OF WOMEN WRITERS

For these new-woman writers argued that "the inner life which questions" must be given full rein. Thus they were avid, not so much for that education achievable by formal schooling, but for consciousness and the knowledge that can follow from it. The premise here is that a woman's life can be her own only if she is first in full possession of her mind. So elementary a point would not seem deserving of emphasis had the writers themselves not insisted upon it. They knew that the ethos of the enthroned "perfect woman" functioned to deny and suppress consciousness, itself the "imaginative power and habit of story-making," as Gilman termed it in "The Yellow Wallpaper," the story in which the rationalist physician-husband drives his wife insane by working to immobilize her, body and mind.

Chopin addresses the problem of consciousness in terms of a primordial state of being. The beginning of the human world "is necessarily vague, tangled, chaotic, and exceedingly disturbing," she writes. "How few of us ever emerge from such a beginning! How many souls perish in its tumult!" In Chopin's terms, to perish, especially in marriage, is to exist without consciousness. Chopin's Edna initially does so, "unthinkingly, as we walk, move, sit, stand, go through the daily treadmill of the life which has been apportioned out to us." This is the woman automaton, in Glasgow's term, "born to decorate instead of to reason." She emerges in Wharton's Anna Leath (*The Reef* [1912]), who spends her childhood in a household in which "the unusual was regarded as either immoral or ill-bred, and people with emotions were not visited." Wharton re-created this figure in May Welland (*The Age of Innocence* [1920]), whose fiancé knows "it was his duty, as a 'decent' fellow, to conceal his past from her, and hers, as a marriageable girl, to have no past to conceal." May is "trained not to possess . . . experience, versatility, freedom of judgment," and is "doomed to thicken," like her mother, "into the same middle-aged image of invincible innocence."

EXPOSING THE "PERFECT" WOMAN

In full revolt against specious "innocence," these writers concerned with the "regionalism" of female consciousness used that consciousness to construct iconoclastic fictions. This diverse group, from Jewett to Wharton, evades any one comprehensive statement on technique, style, or thematic center. Yet to become conscious, to come into being, is to achieve the vision destructive of disabling myths. From Freeman to the young Gertrude Stein, these women writers exposed the myth of the "perfect woman" and thus of its complementary obverse, patriarchy. It is fair to say that consciousness of the new woman stirred all these writers into a fiction of iconoclasm, a scathing indictment of the status quo and the values serving to maintain it.

MARY WILKINS FREEMAN

Freeman, whose productive years began in the 1880s, is an instructive case in point because she could not benefit from the generalized, prevalent new-woman ideology of the 1910s or 1920s and was thus limited in her literary field of action. "Little female weapons," she calls the powers of one of her characters, speaking inadvertently of her own. In the story "Christmas Jenny" (in *A New England Nun*) Freeman warns about the exercise of women's authority in a patriarchal culture. In defense of a neighbor considered to be eccentric, a woman gets so "carried away by affection and indignation" that she "almost spoke in poetry" and, in the eyes of the men, "became so abnormal that she was frightful." Indirectly, Freeman reveals her own literary predicament. The passions of the woman writer must be roused—but formally constrained lest she be judged frightfully abnormal by the devotees of the women's advice books and by the men (rep-

resented by such figures as ministers, lawyers, and proper-
tied farmers) who constitute established power. Literary de-
fiance must not exceed their criteria for normality.

Thus Freeman becomes a covert revolutionist, as a number of her stories reveal, among them "The Village Singer,"
"Sister Liddy," "Christmas Jenny," "A Church Mouse," and
"The Revolt of 'Mother.'" All deal with the triumph of
women's will. Each features a woman whose quiet life con-
ceals "the elements of revolution." Such characters as Can-
dace Whitcomb, Polly Moss, Mrs. Carcy, Hetty Fifield, and
Sarah Penn all revolt. "Men git in a good many places where
they don't belong . . . jest because they push in ahead of
women," says Hetty Fifield ("A Church Mouse"), a homeless
woman who crosses gender roles and, with the support of
community women, claims a place on men's terrain. Sarah
Penn ("The Revolt of 'Mother'") wins a territory of her own
when she moves the family out of their crowded box of a
house into the spacious new barn. Sarah is "overcome with
her own triumph," triumph that, in Freeman's fiction, leaves
the men momentarily disempowered, helpless as Sarah's
weeping husband.

But Freeman limits women's revolution. Or, to put it another way, revolution itself limits Freeman's literary course
of action, given her need not to be offensively "abnormal."
Her insurrectionists, however modest their New England
villages, call for the overturn of the old order and for a re-
formation of society according to the new consciousness
they have brought to themselves and others. Freeman, however, was committed as a writer to "normal," nonfrightening
fiction. (Her most passionate revolutionaries are too old to
incite others to rebellion or to be sexually driven.) Caught in
a formal and thematic dilemma between the status quo and
its threatened overturn, Freeman often preserves the integrity of her insurrectionist women by mooting her own
deepest thematic points.

SARAH ORNE JEWETT

Sarah Orne Jewett, another precursor of the new-woman
movement, also sought acceptable forms in which to assert
the power of woman's consciousness. Jewett's feminist politics took shape when, as a Maine doctor's daughter, she considered the study of medicine and realized the extent of so-
cietal enmity to be incurred by a woman in that or in any

professional role. *A Country Doctor* contains Jewett's mani-
festo of the feminist principles she codified and continued to
follow as a professional writer.

The pastoral treatment of her literary subject matter,
however, formally limited Jewett's new-woman themes. Her
commitment to the conventions of pastoral literature guar-
anteed that Jewett's fiction would not trumpet new-woman
themes in polemical tones. For instance, her acknowledged
masterwork, the novella *The Country of the Pointed Firs*
(1889), divides characters along issues of gender. The men
of the coastal Maine village are superannuated, weak, ad-
dled. In Jewett's world, vision and initiative are the monopoly of the women, especially Almira Todd, the generous,
bountiful, incisive, gregarious, independent, philosophical,
fair-minded *genius loci* of the novella, who stands "grand
and architectural, like a *caryatide*"—more, like an "oracle,"
as both Medea and Antigone. Jewett's country of the pointed
first is, to borrow a title from Charlotte Gilman, "herland."

Yet Jewett's voice never rises to feminist militancy. She
softens her new-woman material by working primarily in
the tradition of the pastoral idyll. "Mrs. Todd might belong to
any age," she writes, "like an idyll of Theocritus." The third
century B.C. Greek poet had depicted the simple, rustic life in
Sicily to please the sophisticated Alexandrians, just as the
well-traveled, worldly Jewett presented rural Maine to
America's urban intelligentsia. Her elegaic tone and her fidelity to the pastoral idyll blunt the new-woman feminist
"principles" Jewett had stated militantly as personal doctrine in *A Country Doctor*. Formally, the idyll makes her a
gentle iconoclast.

By the 1900s, however, the American new-woman writers
were abandoning formal and tonal constraints on consciousness. In *The Age of Innocence*, set in 1870s New York, Wharton brought forth the woman who is literally the embodiment of consciousness itself. The American-born Countess
Ellen Mingott Olenska has "had to look at the Gorgon" and
can never again repose in "blessed darkness." Hers is the
iconoclastic vision that rejects the näiveté of the married
man who wants to flee with her. More experienced than he,
more conscious of the claim of society, she knows that the
social structure turns romance into squalor. The scenes between the two of them throb with sexual energy, but Wharton never retreats from Ellen's sociocultural insights.

KATE CHOPIN'S *THE AWAKENING*

The new-woman iconoclastic consciousness, however, could be problematic, as Chopin's *The Awakening* reveals. The protagonist, Edna Pontellier, a New Orleans businessman's wife and the mother of two young sons, knows she would sacrifice her life but not her self for her children. Edna's route to consciousness includes an unconsummated extramarital love affair, a tryst, and, on Chopin's part, an elaborate use of the sea as a symbol of release from social constraints.

Some readers see Edna as a flamboyant romantic to the end. In this reading a romantic Edna ultimately drowses to her death in a dream of self-fulfillment via romantic Love and Art. According to this interpretation, it is not Edna but the author-narrator who achieves the real awakening into critical analysis of society and romance.

Those who see Edna Pontellier as a triumph of the new-woman consciousness, however, find her to be an iconoclast of romance, motherhood, and marriage because she thinks the unthinkable in authoritative terms that the author supports. Edna thus can function as a figure knowledgeably conscious of a woman's inner life. Discursively she offers the disinterested and authoritative critique of culture, at the same time opening the psyche of the woman and demystifying romance, marriage, and motherhood. To awaken is, by definition, to leave those shibboleths behind. Edna says, "Perhaps it is better to wake up after all, even to suffer, rather than to remain a dupe to illusions all one's life."

The Awakening, however, brings up a crucial problem of the new-woman fiction. Once consciousness is achieved and deployed against pernicious myths, what remains? Beyond iconoclasm, what is the ultimate use of consciousness?

Chopin's novel enacts this problem. In form it argues that beyond awakening there is no transcendence because a woman like Edna is caught in a double bind. In youth she is romantic, but in awakened maturity inevitably jaded. She can do nothing with her hard-won knowledge, her very consciousness. To step beyond the newborn's miasma or off the routinized treadmill of unconsciousness is to enter the world of this bind, which only becomes clear to Edna (and to the reader) in the closing pages of the novel, at which point Edna yields irrevocably to the embrace of the sea, having concluded that there is no transcendence but only a cruel awakening from illusion and the prospect of an unlivable life ahead. The story has enacted the disjunctive movement from romantic illusion to the abyss.

We are meant to see Edna's ultimate, suicidal swim as an existential act in a culturally and psychologically unlivable life. But because ennui prompts it, and because it obliterates Edna's hard-won consciousness, the death-swim focuses the very question of the use of consciousness. Edna becomes, inadvertently on Chopin's part, a precursor to F. Scott Fitzgerald's shallow Daisy Buchanan in *The Great Gatsby*, who asks, "What'll we do with ourselves this afternoon . . . and the day after that, and the next thirty years?" In fact, Chopin had no answer. She had charted Edna's developing consciousness and the knowledge gained from it. After that she did not know what to do. The ostensibly triumphant death-swim, which works at the level of high melodrama, only masks Chopin's dilemma, which is the dilemma of the new-woman writer facing the problem of the burden of consciousness itself.

The iconoclastic new-woman writers engaged this problem in diverse ways. But all asked, How can consciousness be empowering, and what forms can manifest the power of women? This quest for formal structures adequate to the new-woman consciousness took multiple forms, from the diary to the utopian novel and quasi autobiography. The locus of consciousness also varied in the writings of Gilman, Wharton, Glasgow, Cather, and Stein. Seeking alternatives to the urban, industrial, scientific male *Bildungsroman*, these writers also sought alternatives to the cul-de-sac enacted in *The Awakening*, which argued that to come to life as a woman is necessarily to choose death.

Jack London, Upton Sinclair, and the Progressive Movement

Alfred Kazin

The Progressive movement, which dominated public debate in America from 1904–1917, sought to cleanse American business practices and political life of the corruption ushered in after the Civil War. The movement found a political leader in President Theodore Roosevelt, and a literary voice in the writing of Jack London and Upton Sinclair, among others. Upton Sinclair's 1906 novel *The Jungle* is a perfect example of Progressive literature. Sinclair saw literary craft as secondary to the idea of using literature to convey a powerful message that would lead to reform. His horrifying depiction of the Chicago stockyards and processed meat industry led to a public scandal and the passage of regulatory legislation on a national level. However, Alfred Kazin shows that the entire movement was full of contradictions. Progressive reformers sought to curb influence of the country's industrial giants, but at the same time they were drawn to and fascinated by their wealth and power. So while Jack London was a committed socialist reformer, his best writing, such as *The Call of the Wild*, is a romantic celebration of a ruthless natural order where only the strongest survive. Beginning with his classic study of American literature, *On Native Grounds* (1942), Alfred Kazin was one of America's best known and best loved literary critics for over fifty years.

With the turn of the century and the coming of a national interest in reform under the Progressive period, . . . all the forces that had been pressing on the new literature from the late eighties on were suddenly released in a flood, and a mood of active insurgence seized American writing. The long-awaited reckoning with the realities of the new industrial and scientific epoch was at hand, and a spirit of active critical realism, so widespread in popularity that it seemed to come directly from Theodore Roosevelt in the White House, now swept through politics and journalism, gave a new impetus to young realistic novelists, and stimulated American liberal thought to every sphere. . . .

The new spirit was abroad; there was change in the air. And everywhere one saw sudden stirrings in the literature that had been waiting for its charter of freedom—in the profound hunger for fresh leadership that fastened on Roosevelt; in the revulsion against ostentatious wealth that united the novelists of the early nineteen-hundreds; in the endless, excited journalism that now flooded the scene and became the tracts of a new time. The technique of the new social novels was not always subtle and the tone was often shrill; but though many of these writers limited themselves to political ends and were deceived by political appearances, they helped to introduce what was virtually a resurgence in all the avenues of American life. The uneasiness, the hesitant half-hopes, remained; but one thing was now clear: The energies of the new century were no longer arrested; American writing had entered upon the Years of Hope. . . .

THE CONTRADICTORY LIFE OF JACK LONDON

The clue to Jack London's work is certainly to be found in his own turbulent life, and not in his Socialism. He was a Socialist by instinct, but he was also a Nietzschean and a follower of [Darwinist philosopher] Herbert Spencer by instinct. All his life he grasped whatever straw of salvation lay nearest at hand, and if he joined Karl Marx to the Superman with a boyish glee that has shocked American Marxists ever since, it is interesting to remember that he joined Herbert Spencer to [English romantic poet Percy] Shelley, and astrology to philosophy, with as carefree a will. The greatest story he ever wrote was the story he lived: the story of the illegitimate son of a Western adventurer and itinerant astrologer, who grew up in Oakland, was an oyster pirate at fifteen, a sailor at seventeen, a tramp and a "workbeast," a trudger af-

ter Coxey's Army,[1] a prospector in Alaska, and who quickly
became rich by his stories, made and spent several fortunes,
and by the circle of his own confused ambitions came round
to the final despair in which he took his life. That story he
tried to write in all his books—to depict himself in various
phases as the struggling youth in *Martin Eden*, the lonely
stormer of the heavens in *The Sea Wolf*, the triumphant natural man in *The Call of the Wild*, the avenging angel of his
own class in *The Iron Heel*, and even the reprobate drunkard
in *John Barleycorn*. He never succeeded fully, because he
never mastered himself fully. That is easy to say, but London
knew it better than anyone else. He clutched every doctrine,
read and worked nineteen hours a day, followed many directions; in his heart he followed none. . . .

THE "SUPERMAN"

It is the man of power, the aspirant Superman, who bestrides
London's books, now as self-sacrificing as Prometheus, now
as angry as Jove, but always a "blond beast," strangely bearing Jack London's own strength and Jack London's good
looks. His Socialism was in truth an unconscious condescension; he rejoiced in the consciousness of a power which
could be shared by the masses, a power that spilled over
from the leader, as in *The Iron Heel*. His love for the class
from which he sprang was deep enough, but it was a love
founded on pity, the consciousness of common sufferings in
the past; his own loyalty to it was capricious. What he said
of his books he could have said with equal justice of his Socialism: "I have always stood for the exalting of the life that
is in me over art, or any other extraneous thing." For one of
his most powerful books, *The People of the Abyss*, he lived in
London for months as a tramp, searching with the derelicts
for food in the garbage thrown by prosperous householders
into the mud. After reporting on the half-million and more
of those "creatures dying miserably at the bottom of the social pit called London," he quoted with grim approval
Theodore Parker's judgment of half a century before: "England is the paradise of the rich, the purgatory of the wise,
and the hell of the poor." Yet for all his passionate sympathy
with the sufferings of the poor, in England and America, his

---

1. the name given to a march from Ohio to Washington D.C., led by Jacob Coxey, to
protest the poverty brought on by the 1893 economic depression

role as the "first working-class writer" carried no responsibility to the working class with it. He was a working-class writer because the fortunes of that class provided his only major experience; but he had no scruples about cheapening his work when the market for which he wrote compelled him to. Dreiser put it unforgettably when he wrote of London: "He did not feel that he cared for want and public indifference. Hence his many excellent romances.". . .

A WORLD OF STRUGGLE AND VIOLENCE

By 1913 he could boast that he was the best-known and highest-paid writer in the world, and he had reached that eminence by cultivating the vein of Wild West romance. . . . He never believed in any strength equal to his, for that strength had come from his own self-assertion; and out of his worship of strength and force came his delight in violence. He had proved himself by it, as seaman and adventurer, and it was by violence that his greatest characters came to live. For violence was their only avenue of expression in a world which, as London conceived it, was a testing-ground for the strong; violence expressed the truth of life, both the violence of the naturalist creed and the violence of superior men and women. Needless to say, it was London himself who spoke through Wolf Larsen, that Zolaesque Captain Ahab in *The Sea Wolf,* when he said: "I believe that life is a mess. It is like yeast, a ferment, a thing that moves or may move for a minute, an hour, a year, or a hundred years, but that in the end will cease to move. The big eat the little that they may continue to move, the strong eat the weak that they retain their strength. The lucky eat the most and move the longest, that is all." So all his primitive heroes, from Wolf Larsen to Martin Eden and Ernest Everhard, the blacksmith hero of *The Iron Heel,* came to express his desperate love of violence and its undercurrent of romanticism: the prize-fighter in *The Game,* the prehistoric savages in *Before Adam,* the wild dog in *White Fang,* the gargantuan *Daylight in Burning Daylight,* and even the very titles of later books like *The Strength of the Strong* and *The Abysmal Brute.*

THE APPEAL OF LONDON'S WORK

What his immediate contemporaries got out of London, it is now clear, was not his occasional Socialist message, but the same thrill in pursuit of "the strenuous life" that Theodore

Roosevelt gave it. No one before him had discovered the literary possibilities of the Alaskan frontier, and he satisfied the taste of a generation still too close to its own frontier to lack appreciation of "red-blooded" romance, satisfied it as joyfully and commercially as he knew how. How much it must have meant, in a day when Nietzsche's Superman seemed to be wearing high boots and a rough frontiersman's jacket, to read the story of Buck in *The Call of the Wild*, that California dog-king roving in the Alaskan wilderness whom London had conceived as a type of the "dominant primordial beast"! How much it must have meant to polite readers, shivering with delight over "the real thing," to read a sentence like: "Buck got a frothing adversary by the throat, and was sprayed with blood when his teeth sank through the jugular"! Socialism or no Socialism, London appeared in his time as a man who could play all the roles of his generation with equal zest and indiscriminate energy—the insurgent reformer, the follower of Darwin and Herbert Spencer, the naturalist who worked amid romantic scenes, and especially the kind of self-made success, boastful and dominant and contemptuous of others, that at the same time appealed to contemporary taste and frightened it. For if it matters to us, it did not matter to London or his time that intensity is not enough. There was an apocalypse in all his stories of struggle and revolt—it is that final tearing of the bond of convention that London himself was to accomplish only by his suicide—that satisfied the taste for brutality; and nothing is so important about London as the fact that he came on the scene at a time when the shocked consciousness of a new epoch demanded the kind of heady violence that he was always so quick to provide.

Yet a romanticist he remained to the end, with all the raging fury of those who live in a hostile universe. The most popular writer of his generation, London was the loneliest; and for all his hopes of Socialism, personally the most tragic. Rejoicing in his adventure yarns, his own day could not see that the hulking supermen and superbeasts in his novels, while as "real" as thick slabs of bleeding meat, were essentially only a confession of despair. His heroes stormed the heights of their own minds, and shouted that they were storming the world. The early nineteen-hundreds read them as adventurers, symbols of their own muscularity. . . . Like so many novelists in his generation, Socialist though he was,

London wanted only "to get back," to escape into the dream of an earlier and happier society. The joke is that he reminded that generation—as he has still the power to remind us—only of the call men once heard in the wild, the thrill that could still run down a man's spine when there had been a wild, and life was a man-to-man fight, and good.

Was London the almost great writer some have felt in him, a powerful talent born out of his time? Or was he one of those sub-artists who out of the very richness of their personal experience only seem to suggest the presence of art in their work? It is hard to say, and perhaps, if the irony of his career is forgotten, he will be remembered as one of the last Western adventurers, a "pioneer Socialist" novelist, a name in the books, the friend of all those boys who want to run away from home. Yet it is good to remember that in at least one of his books that are still read today, *The Call of the Wild*, Jack London lives forever in the cold clear light of his life's

PROGRESSIVISM AND THE URBAN GHETTOES

Like so many writers of the Realist era, Stephen Crane learned his craft and came in contact with all aspects of urban life as a journalist. In his first novel, Maggie: A Girl of the Streets *(1893), Crane creates an entirely unsentimental portrait of urban poverty, in all its squalor and despair. Realism and the reform impulse came together in the work of writers such as Stephen Crane and the reform-minded journalist Jacob Riis, whose work* How the Other Half Lives *was published in 1890. The American reading public had never before been subjected to such unvarnished portraits of the urban poor and their wretched living conditions.*

Eventually they entered into a dark region where, from a careening building, a dozen gruesome doorways gave up loads of babies to the street and the gutter. A wind of early autumn raised yellow dust from cobbles and swirled it against an hundred windows. Long streamers of garments fluttered from fire-escapes. In all unhandy places there were buckets, brooms, rags and bottles. In the street infants played or fought with other infants or sat stupidly in the way of vehicles. Formidable women, with uncombed hair and disordered dress, gossiped while leaning on railings, or screamed in frantic quarrels. Withered persons, in curious postures of submission to something, sat smoking pipes in obscure corners. A thousand odors of cooking food came forth to the street. The building purpose. For what is it but Jack London's own liberation from the pack of men in their competitive society that Buck, that Nietzschean hound, traces as he runs the pack out to forage alone in the wilderness? There, on the Alaskan heights, was London's greatest burst of splendor, his one affirmation of life that can still be believed. . . .

THE RADICALISM OF UPTON SINCLAIR

Sinclair burst into fame with the most powerful of all the muckraking novels, *The Jungle*, and he has been an irritant to American complacency ever since. His life, with its scandals and its headline excitements, its political excursions and alarums, its extraordinary purity and melodrama, is the story of a religious mission written, often in tabloid screamers, across the pages of contemporary history. As a novelist, he has suffered for his adventures, but it is doubtful if he would have been a novelist without them. The spirit of cru-

---

quivered and creaked from the weight of humanity stamping about in its bowels.

A small ragged girl dragged a red, bawling infant along the crowded ways. He was hanging back, baby-like, bracing his wrinkled, bare legs.

The little girl cried out: "Ah, Tommie, come ahn. Dere's Jimmie and fader. Don't be a-pullin' me back."

She jerked the baby's arm impatiently. He fell on his face, roaring. With a second jerk she pulled him to his feet, and they went on. With the obstinacy of his order, he protested against being dragged in a chosen direction. He made heroic endeavors to keep on his legs, denounce his sister and consume a bit of orange peeling which he chewed between the times of his infantile orations.

As the sullen-eyed man, followed by the blood-covered boy, drew near, the little girl burst into reproachful cries. "Ah, Jimmie, youse bin fightin' agin."

The urchin swelled disdainfully.

"Ah, what deh hell, Mag. See?"

The little girl upbraided him. "Youse allus fightin', Jimmie, an' yeh knows it puts mudder out when yehs come home half dead, an' it's like we'll all get a poundin'."

She began to weep. The babe threw back his head and roared at his prospects.

Reprinted from *Maggie: A Girl of the Streets* in *Prose and Poetry: Stephen Crane* (New York: Library of America, 1984), 11.

sading idealism that gave Sinclair his chance inevitably
made him a perennial crusader as well. . . . What Sinclair
had to give to modern American literature was not any leading ideas as such, but an energy of personal and intellectual
revolt that broke barriers down wherever he passed. At a
time when all the pioneer realists seemed to be aiming at
their own liberation, Sinclair actually helped toward a liberation greater than his own by making a romantic epic out of
the spirit of revolt. From the first he was less a writer than
an example, a fresh current of air pouring through the stale
rooms of the past. Impulsive and erratic as he may have
been, often startlingly crude for all his intransigence, he yet
represented in modern American literature what William
Jennings Bryan represented in modern American politics—
a provincialism that leaped ahead to militancy and came
into leadership over all those who were too confused or too
proud or too afraid to seize leadership and fight for it. . . .

THE BIRTH OF *THE JUNGLE*

Living in great poverty with his wife and young child, hu-
miliated by his obscurity, he wrote out the story of his own
struggles in *The Journal of Arthur Stirling,* the furious romantic confession of a starving young poet who was supposed to have taken his own life at twenty-two. When it was
disclosed that the book was a "hoax" and that Sinclair himself was Stirling, the sensation was over; but the book was
more authentic than anyone at the moment could possibly
know. "The world which I see about me at the present moment," he wrote there in the character of Arthur Stirling,
"the world of politics, of business, of society, seems to me a
thing demoniac in its hideousness; a world gone mad with
pride and selfish lust; a world of wild beasts writhing and
grappling in a pit.". . .

The Jungle saved him. Tiring of romantic novels which no
one would read, he had turned to the investigation of social
conditions, and in his article on "Our Bourgeois Literature,"
in *Collier's,* 1904, he exclaimed significantly: "So long as we
are without heart, so long as we are without conscience, so
long as we are without even a mind—pray, in the name of
heaven, why should anyone think it worthwhile to be troubled because we are without a literature?" Although he still
thought of himself as a romantic rebel against "convention,"
he had come to identify his own painful gropings with the

revolutionary forces in society, and when he received a chance to study conditions in the stockyards at Chicago, he found himself like St. Paul on the road to Damascus. Yet into the story of the immigrant couple, Jurgis and Ona, he poured all the disappointment of his own apprenticeship to life, all, his humiliation and profound ambition. *The Jungle* attracted attention because it was obviously the most authentic and most powerful of the muckraking novels, but Sinclair wrote it as the great romantic document of struggle and hardship he had wanted to write all his life. In his own mind it was above all the story of the betrayal of youth by the America it had greeted so eagerly, and Sinclair recited with joyous savagery every last detail of its tribulations. The romantic indignation of the book gave it its fierce honesty, but the facts in it gave Sinclair his reputation, for he had suddenly given an unprecedented social importance to muckraking. The sales of meat dropped, the Germans cited the book as an argument for higher import duties on American meat, Sinclair became a leading exponent of the muckraking spirit to thousands in America and Europe, and met with the President. No one could doubt it, the evidence was overwhelming: Here in *The Jungle* was the great news story of a decade written out in letters of fire. Unwittingly or not, Sinclair had proved himself one of the great reporters of the Progressive era, and the world now began to look up to him as such.

Characteristically, however, Sinclair spent the small fortune he had received from the book on Helicon Hall, that latter-day Brook Farm[2] for young rebels at which Sinclair Lewis is reported to have been so indifferent a janitor. In his own mind Upton Sinclair had become something more than a reporter; he was a crusader, and after joining with Jack London to found the Intercollegiate Socialist Society, a leading Socialist. "Really, Mr. Sinclair, you *must* keep your head," Theodore Roosevelt wrote to him when he insisted after the publication of *The Jungle* on immediate legislative action. But Sinclair would not wait. If society would not come to him, he would come to society and teach it by his books. With the same impulsive directness that he had converted Jurgis into a Socialist in the last awkward chapter of *The Jungle*, he jumped

2. an alternative utopian farming community that existed in Roxbury, Massachusetts in the 1840s

ahead to make himself a "social detective," a pamphleteer-
novelist whose books would be a call to action. . . .

PROGRESSIVE LITERATURE USED
AS A WEAPON FOR SOCIAL CHANGE

Wherever it was that Sinclair had learned to write millions
of words with the greatest of ease—probably in the days
when he produced hundreds of potboilers—he now wrote
them in an unceasing torrent on every subject that interested
him. Like [reformer] Bronson Alcott and [Populist] William
Jennings Bryan, he had an extraordinary garrulity, and his
tireless and ubiquitous intelligence led him to expose the
outrages of existence everywhere. He used his books for "social purposes" not because he had a self-conscious esthetic
about "art and social purpose," but because his purposes actually were social. Few writers seemed to write less for the
sake of literature, and no writer ever seemed to humiliate
the vanity of literature so deeply by his many excursions
around it. First things came first; the follies of capitalism, the
dangers of drinking, the iniquities of wealthy newspapers
and universities came first. "Why should anyone think it
worthwhile to be troubled because we are without a literature?" His great talent, as everyone was quick to point out,
was a talent for facts, a really prodigious capacity for social
research; and as he continued to give America after the war
the facts about labor in *Jimmie Higgins*, the petroleum industry in *Oil!*, the Sacco-Vanzetti case in *Boston*, Prohibition
in *The Wet Parade*, it mattered less and less that he repeated
himself endlessly, or that he could write on one page with
great power, on another with astonishing self-indulgence
and sentimental melodrama. He had become one of the
great social historians of the modern era.

CHAPTER 4

National Character in American Realism

American
Realism

Realism and Regional Voices

Eric J. Sundquist

Regionalism came into being in America at the same time as Realism. It emphasized the speech, customs and history of a particular area of the United States, whether it was the South, the West, the Midwest, or New England. Because it sought to portray a way of life and language honestly and without exaggeration, sensationalism, or stylistic excess, Regionalism has an obvious relation to the literary aspirations of Realism as outlined by Howells, James and Twain. In the past, critics have tended to privilege Realism at the expense of Regionalism. However, Eric Sundquist argues that Regionalism and Realism were entangled in complex ways, since both literatures were so completely engaged in the immense social and economic changes sweeping through America in the decades following the Civil War. Eric J. Sundquist is a Professor of English at Northwestern University. He has published and edited a number of important books on American literature, including *Home as Found: Authority and Genealogy in Nineteenth Century American Literature* (1979), *Faulkner: The House Divided* (1983), and *To Wake the Nations: Race in the Making of American Literature* (1993).

Because their edges blur and their central meanings shift, the categories "realism" and "regionalism" cannot be conveniently separated. A simple division between the urban realism that accompanied the growth of industrial America in the post-Civil War period and the several regional literatures that flourished at the same time would lose sight of the complex aesthetic, social, and economic entanglements between them. If we instead judge realism from the 1870s through the early 1900s as a developing series of responses to the transformation of land into capital, of raw materials into products, of agrarian values into urban values, and of private experience into public property, then the city appears as one region among others, part of the national network of modernization actualized as much by the ties of language and literature as by new railroad lines and telegraph wires.

The transformation from muscle to mechanical power, wrote Josiah Strong in *The Twentieth Century City* (1898), "has separated, as by all impassable gulf, the simple, homespun, individualistic life of the world's past, from the complex, closely associated life of the present." By the same token, he noted, it now takes sixty-four men to make a shoe. Such ironic complication in modern life can be observed throughout the fiction of the period, which records a revolutionary change in the order of life comparable to that depicted by the great European and Russian novelists of the period. In the United States, as in parts of Europe, the nineteenth century was both an era of industrial progress and heightened materialism, and one of great colonial movements and migrations. In the case of America, this involved heavy European immigration and significant movements of the population from rural to urban areas in the East and Midwest; whereas the West experienced the significant immigration of Asian laborers and the continued dispossession of former Mexican landholders in the aftermath of the 1848 war. The growth of communication and transportation following the Civil War linked the regions of the country and made them newly aware of differences in speech and customs. Vernacular writing by Mark Twain, Sarah Orne Jewett, Hamlin Garland, and others is one manifestation of the variously held American theory (reflecting that of [philosopher] Hippolyte Taine in France) that realistic literature must embody the race, the milieu, and the historical moment of its author. In their often nostalgic attention to diverse regional customs eroded by standardized urban society, American regionalists share with European writers of the period like Thomas Hardy, Ivan Turgenev, and Knut Hamsun the belief that a work's "realism" resides both in its local details and in the larger transfigurations of national ideology to which it responds. . . .

THE RURAL-URBAN CONTRAST

Howells's novels built around the contrast between rural, familial values and urban, corporate values echo the portrayal in much of the period's regional fiction of a sense of crisis or loss, a breakdown in the comparatively close-knit communities of pre-Civil War America in a world increasingly defined by calculated zones of time and labor, and technologies of measurement and regulation, the sparsely populated, flawlessly sketched landscapes of the local colorists came to seem a lost world. The combined aura of timelessness and irrevocable decay that marks the genre's New England masterpiece, Sarah Orne Jewett's *The Country of the Pointed Firs* (1896), appears to the west in Hamlin Garland's *Main-Travelled Roads* (1891), and achieves a brilliant apotheosis in Willa Cather's *My Ántonia* (1920). As a literature of memory, local color often has elements of the historical novel; yet it strives to delineate not history's great figures or movements but the scant record of time's passage left when a simpler way of life succumbs to one more complex.

NEW ENGLAND REALISM

In the fiction of the most important New England local colorists, Sarah Orne Jewett and Mary Wilkins Freeman, memory is often lodged in the vestiges of a world of female domesticity. The country's internal migration of younger men and women to new urban areas has left behind a ghost world of spinsters, widows, and bereft sea captains. Myth, colloquial narratives, and riveting emotion animate Jewett's work, creating in her Maine landscapes an effect of natural simplicity merged with exquisite craft: a scene of trout-fishing in "The Dunnet Shepherdess," an epilogue story to *The Country of the Pointed Firs*, suggests nothing so much as Ernest Hemingway, in whom local color sentiment and the shock of modernist realism would be combined in the next generation.

In the preface to her early collection of stories, *Deephaven* (1877), Jewett speaks of her desire to find "some trace of the lives which were lived among the sights we see and the things we handle." Widely read in European literature and later a figure in Boston literary circles, Jewett nevertheless devoted her writing life to recording the traces—formal customs, speech, legends, everyday habits and manners—of a native American life disappearing from view. She did so by publishing her stories in the nation's leading magazines after the initial encouragement of Howells (who wrote her, "Your voice is like a thrush's in the din of all the literary noises that stun us so"). Her work is thus representative of a paradoxical effect of much local color writing, namely, that the same communication and transportation developments that closed the nation's sectional divisions following the Civil War and brought isolated communities closer also began to destroy rural "islands" of life. Local color records in part the rustic border world rendered exotic by industrialism but now made visible and nostalgically charged by the nation's inexorable drive toward cohesion and standardization.

Also praised by Howells (for her resemblance to Turgenev), Freeman surpasses Jewett in her ability to combine contemporary social problems with a stylistically detailed apprehension of regional character. In the most representative stories in A *Humble Romance* (1887) and *A New England Nun* (1891), a latter-day Puritanism can destroy emotional growth but result as well in ambivalent power among the women who are most often its victims. "A New England Nun," "Sister Liddy" and "The Revolt of 'Mother'" portray the determined resistance of women to pain inflicted upon them by foolish or crude men. Her novel *Pembroke* (1894) stands between Hawthorne's stories and Edith Wharton's brilliant New England works, *Ethan Frome* (1911) and *Summer* (1917), as a study of the "dreadful warping of a diseased will" that tears apart two lovers and their families. *The Portion of Labor* (1901) belongs to the popular genre of labor-romance novels also written by Howells, Isaac K. Friedman, Winston Churchill, and others during the period. Those, like Freeman's, especially concerned with the family and the lives of women can be traced to Rebecca Harding Davis's uncanny industrial romances, *Life in the Iron Mills* (1861) and *Margret Howth* (1862), Louisa May Alcott's *Work* (1873) and more pedestrian sentimental novels like Elizabeth Phelps's *The Silent Partner* (1871) and Amanda Douglas's *Hope Mills* (1880). The heroine of *The Portion of Labor* is a young girl who resembles little Eva in *Uncle Tom's Cabin* in her childhood awareness of "the awful shadow of the labor and poverty of the work world," and she thus represents an overt translation of the abolitionist benevolence Stowe's child heroine had made famous into the new arena of industrial "wage-slavery," and of the archetypes of antebellum romance into the social realism of America's emerging cities.

Comparable to Jewett and Freeman in her use of local setting and manners is the Tennessee writer Mary Murfree, who wrote under the pseudonym Charles Egbert Craddock.

Her popular story "The Dancin' Party at Harrison's Cave" appeared in Howells's *Atlantic* in 1878 and was collected in *In the Tennessee Mountains* (1884). Like other regional work both in the South and in New England, Murfree's sought to record local material threatened with extinction. Her several dozen stories and eight novels combined careful research with tall-tale humor, often depicting the proud and superstitious lives of Tennessee mountain dwellers. *The Prophet of the Great Smoky Mountains* (1885) verges on natural mysticism, while *In the "Stranger People's" Country* (1891) displays the archaeological stance of much local color in its tale of an urban outsider whose study of the burial ground of prehistoric mountain pygmies leads to an involvement in a local romantic rivalry. Murfree's fiction, along with Jewett's,

HAMLIN GARLAND'S ADVOCACY OF REGIONALISM

Aside from his fictional portraits of Midwestern life and the hardships of farming, Hamlin Garland was his generation's most articulate spokesman for Regionalist or (as he termed it) Local Color fiction. Garland's advocacy of fiction that represents local characters and conditions in a language shorn of sentiment and exaggeration illustrates how closely allied the Regionalist movement was to the aims of Realism.

Local color in fiction is demonstrably the life of fiction. It is the native element, the differentiating element. It corresponds to the endless and vital charm of individual peculiarity. It is the differences which interest us; the similarities do not please, do not forever stimulate and feed as do the differences. Literature would die of dry rot if chronicled the similarities only, or even largely. . . .

To-day we have in America, at last, a group of writers who have no suspicion of imitation laid upon them. Whatever faults they may be supposed to have, they are at any rate, themselves. American critics can depend upon a characteristic American literature of fiction and the drama from these people.

The corn has flowered, and the cotton-boll has broken into speech.

Local color—what is it? It means that the writer spontaneously reflects the life which goes on around him. It is natural and unstrained art. . . .

I assert it is the most natural thing in the world for a man to love his native land and his native, intimate surroundings. Born into a web of circumstances, enmeshed in common life, offers a window into secluded territory receding into a past paradoxically contemporaneous with the urban worlds of Howells and Crane. With Garland and Bret Harte in the West, Murfree and Jewett defined local color as a fictional region at once curiously alien and yet entirely familiar to the native American imagination.

THE POST–CIVIL WAR SOUTH

The South stands apart from other regions in that the history of its literature from the end of the Civil War to the early 1900s is of necessity an account of continued sectional pride, conflict with the laws and customs imposed on it during Reconstruction by a Northern government, and participation in the slow process of national healing. Like that of New En-

the youthful artist begins to think. All the associations of that childhood and the love-life of youth combine to make that web of common affairs, threads of silver and beads of gold; the near-at-hand things are the dearest and sweetest after all.

As the reader will see, I am using local color to mean something more than a forced study of the picturesque scenery of a State.

Local color in a novel means that is has such quality of texture and back-ground that it could not have been written in any other place or by any one else than a native.

It means a statement of life as indigenous as the plant-growth. It means that the picturesque shall not be seen by the author,—that every tree and bird and mountain shall be dear and companionable and necessary, not picturesque; the tourist cannot write the local novel.

From this it follows that local color must not be put in for the sake of local color. It must go in, it *will* go in, because the writer naturally carries it with him half unconsciously, or conscious only of its significance, its interest to him.

He must not stop to think whether it will interest the reader or not. He must be loyal to himself, and put it in because he loves it. If he is an artist, he will make his reader feel it through his own emotion.

What we should stand for is not universality of theme, but beauty and strength of treatment, leaving the writer to choose his theme because he loves it.

Reprinted from Hamlin Garland, *Crumbling Idols: Twelve Essays on Art Dealing Chiefly With Literature, Painting and the Drama* (Cambridge MA: The Belknap Press of Harvard University Press, 1960), 49–55.

gland, the South's literature is also one of memory, although in its case the remembered way of life disappeared in a bloody military defeat, never to return in actuality but often to return over the next century in the magnificent dreams probed with both tragic sympathy and devastating irony by such writers as Mark Twain, William Faulkner, and Robert Penn Warren. . . .

OLD SOUTH VERSUS NEW SOUTH

The most popular Southern writer, throughout all parts of the country, was the Georgian Joel Chandler Harris. His newspaper sketches of a former slave named Uncle Remus, who narrated the tales of Brer Rabbit and Brer Fox, grew into a brilliant exploration of black dialect and folklore that generated an immediate, more ironic reply in [Charles] Chesnutt's Uncle Julius in *The Conjure Woman* and would influence later writers like William Faulkner and Ralph Ellison and permeate American popular culture. The stories of Uncle Remus, collected in such volumes as *Uncle Remus: His Songs and Sayings* (1881), *Nights with Uncle Remus* (1883), and *Uncle Remus and His Friends* (1892), do not entirely whitewash the Old South but maintain a taut balance between minstrel humor and a subversive critique of slavery and racism. While Harris's other short fiction and novels— for example, *Free Joe and Other Georgian Sketches* (1887) and *Gabriel Tolliver* (1902)—speak with moderation of Reconstruction and its aftermath, the Uncle Remus stories offer an instance of popular work grounded in local folklore that is more psychologically revealing than sophisticated narrative and speaks with an authentic and original American voice.

At once Southern and cosmopolitan, New Orleans produced some of the nation's best literature in the last decades of the century. The work of Grace King collected in *Balcony Stories* (1893); the Cajun stories of Kate Chopin in *Bayou Folk* (1894) and her lyric novel of discovered sexual freedom, *The Awakening* (1899); and Lafcadio Hearn's beautifully evocative Gulf Coast novel *Chita* (1889) all combine regional materials with artistic craft. Hearn's New Orleans and Caribbean sketches, along with his several important volumes of tales based on the folk stories of Japan, show the merging of *fin-de-siècle* aestheticism with local color's precise observation. Most notable of the New Orleans writers,

however, is George Washington Cable, a Confederate caval-
ryman who wrote successfully in several fields and genres.
His 1885 argument for black rights in "The Freedman's Case
in Equity"—a view expanded the same year in *The Silent
South* and later in *The Negro Question* (1890)—aroused the
indignation of Southerners; and his publication of slave and
Creole musical scores had an important impact on the development of American jazz. Both the commitment to equality and the painstaking interest in local customs mark Cable's fiction as well. Like his stories in *Old Creole Days*
(1879), and his nonfiction in *The Creoles of New Orleans*
(1884), his novels were often based on hours of research
into municipal records and newspapers. His great work, *The
Grandissimes* (1880), is set before the Civil War, a strategy
Twain also employed in *Adventures of Huckleberry Finn* and
Puddn'head Wilson in order to measure ironically the similarities between antebellum slavery and postwar racial conflict. Its dense social texture, its violent tale of miscegenation
and fratricidal betrayal, its lurid account of Bras-Coupé, an
African king reduced to humiliating bondage as an American slave—all these elements raise the novel above sheer regional interest and, as later in Faulkner, suggest an intensi-
fication into mythic, psychological realism. . . .

THE FRONTIER WEST AND MANIFEST DESTINY

Hamlin Garland . . . represents in his fiction the conflict of a
native reservoir of land with a modern commercial order.
His lecture "Local Color in Fiction," for example, was deliv-
ered at the 1893 World's Columbian Exposition in Chicago,
where technology and America's great natural resources
were equally celebrated. Garland's lecture may have been a
less significant event than Frederick Jackson Turner's ex-
pounding of his famous frontier thesis in the same arena, yet
it too marks symbolically the union of the agrarian and urban traditions in a city and on an occasion that quickly became symbolic of America's cultural and industrial progress.

    The Western tradition of which Garland is a more com-
plex exponent can be traced to frontier writing early in the
century, but its first representative in the age of realism is
Bret Harte, whose brief career coincided with the nation's
fascination with a West opened up by the transcontinental
railroad in 1869. The editor of the *Overland Monthly* in California, Harte became famous overnight in 1868 with pic-

turesque gold-country stories like "The Luck of Roaring Camp" and "The Outcasts of Poker Flat," and was able to command from Howells the royal sum of $10,000 in 1871 for work in the *Atlantic*. He helped to create a lasting audience for dime western novels as well as for historical romances of American Indian and pioneer conflict like Helen Hunt Jackson's *Ramona* (1884). In his use of local dialect and landscape he also initiated the vogue of Western "local color" that by the end of the century would be the subject of highly stylized satire in Crane's "The Bride Comes to Yellow Sky" (1898) and "The Blue Hotel" (1899). During the same period the West Coast also witnessed the significant development of an often oppressed Asian community, whose urban experience was first recorded in the short stories collected in *Mrs. Spring Fragrance* (1912), by the British-born Chinese American Edith Maud Eaton writing under the pen name Sui Sin Far.

From the Homestead Act of 1862 through the ascendance of Theodore Roosevelt, the West embodied the dream of America's Manifest Destiny and defined the nation's political and economic course in critical ways. Goaded by gold-inflicted debts, railroad corruption, and fears of corporate manipulation and foreign conspiracy, the Populists of the early 1800s both embodied and capitalized on the failure of America's garden utopia, the lost Jeffersonian world fallen prey to industrial advances. Out of this despair came powerful revitalist-tinged writing that challenged the pastoral ideal. But by the end of the century the agricultural and industrial recovery, along with the nationalist pride evoked by the Spanish-American War, gave the West a fresh mythic dimension exemplified in the raw power of Frank Norris's *McTeague* (1899) and *The Octopus* (1901), the Western landscape writing of Joaquin Miller, John Wesley Powell, and John Muir, such masculine adventure tales as Richard Harding Davis's *Soldiers of Fortune* (1897), and Theodore Roosevelt's celebration of Anglo-Saxon virtues in *The Winning of the West* (1889) and *The Strenuous Life* (1900). . . .

To the extent that the new Anglo-Saxonism arose from the territorial conquests of the Mexican War anti directly influenced attitudes toward later immigrants, especially East European Jews crowding into New York, the idea of the "West" can be understood in the context of growing debate over the power of the supposedly superior race to determine the course of American destiny. But it may also be viewed as an arena for the struggle between economic progress and fading ideals of male independence and self-reliance. Owen Wister's *The Virginian* (1902), dedicated to Roosevelt, portrays the vanished world not of Eastern America but of nineteenth-century Wyoming. Yet its tale of the naturally aristocratic cowboy transplanted from Virginia to the West makes his courage, his enterprise, and his rugged individualism the signs of a true democracy disappearing under pressure from corporate and alien forces.

LIFE ON MIDWESTERN FARMS

Equally influential in the development of a regionalist aesthetic was the group of Midwestern writers whose work leads toward Booth Tarkington's elegiac drama, *The Magnificent Ambersons* (1918), and Sinclair Lewis's stinging satire, *Main Street* (1920). The first of them was the circuit rider and Bible salesman Edward Eggleston, whom Garland would call "the father of us all." His novels, influenced by Taine's theories of race and milieu, show a careful attention to the dialect and manners of frontier Indiana, Illinois, and Ohio. *The Hoosier Schoolmaster* (1871) and *The Circuit Rider* (1874) are for the most part adventurous entertainments; but *The End of the World* (1872) and *Roxy* (1878) are striking critiques of religious fanaticism. An influential Chicago literary figure who wrote significant histories of that city, Joseph Kirkland was also praised by the younger Garland, who thought his fiction "as native to Illinois" as Tolstoy and Turgenev were to Russia, and who sought him out in Chicago when starting his own career. Kirkland's *Zury* (1887) and its sequel *The McVeys* (1888) are enlivened by the coarse prairie language of their hero, Usury Prouder, whose greed teaches a Populist lesson: "Money-making . . . is like climbing a chimney that grows narrower toward the top; one reaches a place where he can get neither up nor down, and is enveloped in dirt and darkness till he dies." An even darker picture of Midwestern life appears in the work of Kansas newspaperman Edgar Watson Howe, whose eerie *The Story of a Country Town* (1884) looks forward to Sherwood Anderson and Carson McCullers without rising to their level of craft. Malice and insanity pervade this tale of a failed agrarian dream, which was based on Howe's own memories and observations of small-town rural America and elicited the praise of Howells, Twain, and Garland. Howe's brutal picture of family betrayal and psychic collapse is moderated, however, in the formally experimental *A Man Story* (1888) and *The Anthology of Another Town* (1920), as well as the autobiographical memoir *Plain People* (1929).

HAMLIN GARLAND

The achievement of Hamlin Garland that crowned the Midwestern realist tradition was based on his theory of "veritism" articulated in *Crumbling Idols* (1894). The essays in that volume heralded the native qualities of local color and demanded that American literature, in order to be both great and national, "deal with conditions peculiar to our own land and climate." Garland's aesthetic follows Whitman in calling for a democratic art that breaks with corrupt and dying European traditions in order to explore the "new fields" of Midwestern and Far Western America. His theories drew strength from memories of his youth, when his family migrated from Maine to Wisconsin (where Garland was born) to Minnesota to Iowa and finally to South Dakota. But that experience also showed him the bitter toil and loneliness of rural life. Exacerbated by the guilt he felt about leaving his family to move to Boston in 1884, the difficulty of Garland's escape from rural hardship became the theme of his best fiction, which was warmly promoted by Howells and collected in *Main-Travelled Roads* (1891) and *Prairie Folk* (1893). Just as his criticism may be seen as the next step from Howells's "commonplace" realism to the unguarded exploration of hardship and vice by the naturalists, Garland's short fiction, in wrenching stories like "A Branch Road," "Up the Coulee," or "Lucretia Burns," depicts common life in the combined humility and degradation that he would recall from an 1887 return visit to South Dakota: "'The houses, bare as boxes, dropped on the treeless plains, the barbed-wire fences running at tight angles, and the towns mere assemblages of flimsy wooden sheds with painted-pine battlement, produced on me the effect of an almost helpless and sterile poverty.'". . .

With Crane, Garland may be said to have carried forward Howells's realist aesthetic. He introduced the "gaunt, grim, sordid, pathetic, ferocious figures" (as Howells wrote in his review of *Main-Travelled Roads*) that the next generation of writers would take as their central characters, and he recorded with panoramic intensity and acute historical consciousness the dissolution of America's Western garden. . . .

THE TENSIONS OF AMERICAN REGIONALISM

The small towns or farms left behind by the protagonists of Garland, Howells, . . . or Dreiser when they come to the new cities of iron and glass live as flickering memories, signs of a seemingly vanished order. In the journey between the regions of rural and urban life, most of all in the tension that binds them together, lies the substance and spirit of American realism. Held in balance by the emerging techniques of industrial labor, by racial and class antagonism, and by the twin energies of commerce and social progress, the period's fiction speaks eloquently of the moral complexity and paradoxical freedoms of modern American life. In that fiction what is "real" resists easy categorization but belongs instead to the rich profusion and often idiosyncratic detail of the diverse regional and ethnic voices of which America was being composed.

The Image of the Frontier in American Realism

James K. Folsom

Many critics have noted the power and presence of the frontier in the imaginations of a range of American writers. The American frontier presented new opportunities and the chance for individual regeneration and success, and therefore functioned as a symbol of the American Dream. It also functioned as a boundless space where the increasingly populated Eastern seaboard could send its excess population and thereby relieve social tensions. James K. Folsom argues that, for Realist writers, the frontier functioned as an image or idea as much as it did a geographical space. The frontier was not so important for what it was but for what it meant, and it came to mean more than simply the "West" and the "Western Literature" it produced. Increasingly, it came to symbolize any new, mysterious space that had to be understood and absorbed into the imagination. For example, Europe presented for Henry James a kind of frontier, as more and more Americans traveled there after the Civil War and encountered its complex class system, rules, and rituals. When Howells moved from Ohio to the East, the complex and growing cities of Boston and New York presented themselves to him as new frontiers that his Western consciousness had to comprehend. James K. Folsom taught literature at the University of Colorado and wrote extensively on Western American Literature.

On the face of things, Americans' preoccupation with the frontier and literature about it during the Gilded Age (I use the term "Gilded Age" to refer to that period in American history between the Civil War and World War I) is evident. Popular writing forsakes its roots in the Crockett almanacs and the humorists of the Old Southwest to develop into the dime novel, set preponderantly in the West;[1] the locale of Western fiction follows the successive stages of the American frontier; Mark Twain, the author usually viewed as the greatest single voice Western American literature has produced, is a product of the period, as well as the author of the sobriquet "Gilded Age" for it, and the Western, in its modern form, is defined toward the end of the Gilded Age, most importantly by Owen Wister in *The Virginian*, but also by Zane Grey, especially in *Riders of the Purple Sage*. At the same time, the unromantic West of the farm and small town appears as symbol of the often harsh reality rather than the romance of Western American life following the Civil War.

A SOCIAL AND IMAGINATIVE SAFETY VALVE

During this period as well American social historians develop the idea, based originally on the so-called Teutonic theory of democratic origins and culminating in the famed frontier hypothesis of Frederick Jackson Turner, that the presence of the frontier is the single most important fact distinguishing America from its European progenitors. Long before Turner, a relatively unsophisticated statement of his basic idea—that the frontier served as a safety valve for removing dangerous pressures from the society behind it—seemed so self-evident to late nineteenth-century Americans as scarcely to require proof. This notion also explains many literary developments during the Gilded Age and is by no means limited to writings which we have traditionally termed Western.

The Gilded Age also marks the emergence of the United States as an industrial giant, a world economic power rather than a provincial backwater. Brother Jonathan, as the infant United States had demeaningly been referred to, is transformed into Uncle Sam, a figure to be reckoned with, if not always approved of. If, as one plausible etymology suggests, the name Uncle Sam is based on the dollar sign, we are back again to the frontier myth, the long way around: for the omnipotence of the almighty dollar, which as much as any

1. The Crockett almanacs mythologized the life of Davy Crockett in the 1830s and 1840s. Dime novels were cheap, mass produced, and highly sensationally "Western."

single factor created American cultural unease during the period, was often interpreted as the result of an ill-defined Eastern conspiracy to crush the noblemen of nature living in the West. Just as American political dissent in the period was primarily a Western phenomenon—it is no accident that the most famous dissident voice of the Gilded Age belonged to a Nebraskan—so artistic dissent often expressed itself in terms of Western values, even when not specifically Western in subject-matter.

The gradual redefinition of the nature of the conflict in the American Civil War, culminating in the so-called "moonlight and magnolia" school of writing, offers a convenient example. The myth of the antebellum South, like most myths of a Golden Age, does not purport to present sober historical truth: in this myth the romantic South, rather than being visualized as a particular place in a specific historic era, is conceived primarily as representative of a complex of values standing in opposition to those often shoddy values of finance capitalism which dominate the reader's real-life world. Simon Legree[2] disappears: in his place stands the benevolent figure of Ole Massa, beloved of all, including his black slaves. Life on the old plantation becomes a bucolic idyll, destroyed by the Yankees for no good reason. In this fiction the South normally loses the Civil War not because of moral delinquency, let alone military ineptitude or political incompetence, but simply because it is overwhelmed by a gigantic and ruthless enemy armed with greenbacks rather than swords and pistols.

PURIFICATION AND REGENERATION

Several years ago [critic] David B. Davis indicated the resemblances between the myth of the antebellum South and the myth of the West, which "purified and regenerated" the original myth "by the casting off of apologies for slavery." In terms of the present discussion, both the South and the West represented ideals opposed to "the peculiar social and economic philosophy of the Northeast" values "beyond the utilitarian and material." If we expand Davis's line of reasoning, we may suggest that American fascination with both imaginative locales is essentially a fascination with the myth of

---

2. the cruel slaveowner who beats Tom to death in Harriet Beecher Stowe's *Uncle Tom's Cabin* (1852)

the frontier: somewhere must be a land of heart's desire, un-tainted by the commercial values of the present. The re-gional West itself is not particularly important to [journalist and social critic] Horace Greeley's oft-quoted maxim, "Go West, young man, go West." More basic is the idea that an unbearable present may be redeemed by changing one's sit-uation and starting over.

Perhaps this explains as well as any single thing the Amer-ican fascination with the frontier in the Gilded Age. For the Gilded Age was nothing if not a restless one. As the disparity between the promises of America and the realities of late nineteenth-century American life grew more obvious, Amer-ican writers often opted for a world of ideals rather than of unpromising realities. "Frequently sold," as a familiar con-temporary song had it, the American nonetheless continued the search for the good life, wherever it might lead.

OTHER FRONTIERS IN AMERICAN REALISM

It did not always lead west, as Henry James, the literary giant of the period who stands at first glance most directly opposed to Twain, shows. In James's world the land of opportunity, the "last frontier," if one will, is generally Europe. The Amer-ican abroad, although by no means a novel figure at the be-ginning of the Gilded Age, develops new complexity in the work of this fictional master of the "international subject." James's questing characters, although they may not know specifically what they hope to find abroad, know that in a general way they are searching for life, something they seem unable to find in the comfortable down-home existence that surrounds them. The possibilities of their lives at home seem suddenly too limited, and they seek the challenge of a new environment where opportunities are less confined. When occasionally James turns his international subject around, the Europeans visiting America—as in the short novel *The European*—also feel, more in accord with our own historic expectations, the need for a New World in which they may find more opportunities than they had had in the Old.

Yet no matter which way James's characters cross the At-lantic, they do so for essentially the same reasons: to find a new frontier in which their potential can be realized. What they find is a land remarkably like the one they have left be-hind. As the Baroness remarks at the end of *The Europeans,* "Europe seems to me much larger than America."

The ironies which reside in the notion of the "new start" fill James's fiction from the beginning until the end of his career. One irony, of course, is that in one sense beginning anew is impossible, since one always brings one's own self along. More basic to James's world, however, is that the people one meets abroad are virtually indistinguishable from those one has, presumably forever, left behind. In *The Portrait of a Lady* Isabel Archer finds one titled Englishman as a possible suitor, but finally marries—unhappily, it is true—a denationalized American. Her circle of friends in Europe contains relatively few Europeans. This may well be a Jamesian barb at the propensity of Americans abroad to associate almost entirely with their own countrymen and -women, but Isabel Archer's fruitless quest indicates as well James's immersion in American frontier mythology—the search for a better land somewhere beyond the limits of the known, and the disillusionment this search must entail.

WOMEN AND THE WEST

It is no accident that James's questing Americans are so often female. The frontier myth in its typically Wild Western format is almost entirely a male myth. Although one may not totally agree with Davis's statement that the Eastern belle in the typical Western is "a glorified horse" his general point that female characters are almost always stereotypical in one way or another is well taken. Kansas, or Oklahoma, or wherever, was, according to the old wheeze, tough on women and horses, and the comparison, unflattering as it may be, contains a grain of truth. Horace Greeley knew what he was doing when he suggested that young men go west, for the West, unless one were brawny and physically robust, was not a land of opportunity. Young women would have been better advised to follow Isabel Archer to Europe or Dreiser's Carrie Meeber to Chicago. No matter what one might find in the fleshpots of Chicago, let alone Europe, it would be better than what one got by remaining at home. [Regionalist writer] Mary E. Wilkins Freeman's New England nun, living out her days in a moribund New England village, is in a worse plight than any of her more venturesome sisters.

THE DARK SIDE OF WESTWARD EXPANSION

Just as James's frontiers are not specifically Western ones, so other American writers often chronicle what are essentially the concerns of frontier mythology in works which are not, when considered strictly in terms of subject matter, directly concerned with the American West. Hank Morgan, the Yankee of Twain's consistently under-praised *A Connecticut Yankee in King Arthur's Court*, is a case in point. Among its other concerns this novel records what is almost an allegorical demonstration of the negative effects of American westward expansion: the Yankee, armed with all the technological prowess of nineteenth-century America, brings the benefits of civilization to a frontier populated by a group of amiable savages. The benefits he brings turn out not only to be prophetic of America's new role as a world power but also agents in the destruction of the natives to whom he brings them. This novel, as well as any literary work of the period, shows the double-edged quality of the American's frontier vision: the quest for a new start, what Oswald Spengler would later name the Faustian vision of Western man, is hailed as a virtue, while the results of this Faustian quest are seen as disastrous.

FRONTIER UTOPIAS AND DYSTOPIAS

Edward Bellamy's *Looking Backward*, the most widely read utopian novel ever penned, affords another convenient example. Although the primary concern of this work is to demonstrate the present ills of late nineteenth-century society and to suggest a future cure for them, the vehicle of Bellamy's parable is saturated with frontier ideals. Bellamy's utopia is conceived as a place free of the disagreeable qualities of nineteenth-century industrial life, yet located geographically in the same area. What more graphic illustration of the promise of the frontier—and by extension of America—could be imagined than Bellamy's city of the future sited on the remains of the past, where the evils of the present have been eradicated and where mankind's restless spirit is at last satisfied.

Frontier writing has of necessity always contained a strong utopian component, but in the Gilded Age the predominant utopias are negative ones, dystopias, as they have come to be known, more on the model of Twain than of Bellamy. The optimistic vision which redeems them, as at the end of *Looking Backward*, normally seems unreal, a product more of wishful thinking than of careful examination of the evidence. Ignatius Donnelly's *Caesar's Column*, more typical of the mass of utopian novels than *Looking Backward*, is memorable primarily for its pictures of the frustration and despair of society's members rather than for the rays of hope with which Donnelly, himself a prominent political figure, attempts to paint it. Indeed, even in *Looking Backward* the multiple shifts in time with which Bellamy brings about his happy ending have struck many readers as absurd. In any event, the idea of a frontier is of primary importance to this novel and, Turner to the contrary, the last frontier can never, literally at least, be reached.

EAST VERSUS WEST

It is also in the Gilded Age that our modern view of Western and Eastern values as diametrically opposed becomes clearly articulated. Earlier fiction had denied a basic conflict between them or, if the conflict was theoretically admitted, had done its best to gloss over it. . . . For the Gilded Age the Westerner is a valuable member of society in his own right, and it is his values which will redeem that society. For the first time in the Gilded Age the modern imaginative theme clearly emerges that the West will redeem the East, instead of the more traditional idea that the East will reform the West in its own image. The change is, of course, not absolute and the tension between the older vision of the West as East manque[3] and the newer that the two are essentially opposed is felt throughout Western writing of the period, not always with the most fortunate results. Many readers have felt that the change in Owen Wister's Virginian from reckless cowboy to budding entrepreneur is one of the weakest features of *The Virginian;* and Hamlin Garland, to use a very different example, never seems to be quite sure whether the misfortune in his tales is primarily the fault of some representative of Eastern values or simply due to the hardships of Western life. In "Under the Lion's Paw" he argues the former case; in "Up the Coule" the latter; in *A Spoil of Office* and *The Moccasin Ranch* he is not quite sure.

The primary significance of the emergence of this modern notion that Western and Eastern values are essentially opposed again reflects the vast changes in American life following the Civil War and, more important for this discussion, the feeling that the East had abandoned that questing spirit which Westerners still possessed. If in Western writing

3. a "lost" East

Eastern and Western values are visualized in conflict, this is primarily, to Western eyes at least, a result of the East's having lost the idea of the West that the West itself still retains. This being the case, abandonment of frontier values is tantamount to renunciation of ones American identity.

This, it seems to me, is a major thrust of the Turner hypothesis, and it is unfortunate that Western Americanists, with their eyes fixed upon the presence of the physical frontier, have by and large overlooked it. For to Turner the frontier in itself is not an especially desirable place. In his view, the first wave of settlers has a hard enough time living at all even to think of living well. The primary significance of the frontier for him lies in its effect upon the society behind it, which is constantly revitalized by its impact. Going native is not Turner's idea of the good life. Instead, the presence of the frontier represents a force which constantly rejuvenates an American society that, left to itself, would become constantly more over-refined and decadent.

RURAL STAGNATION AND WESTERN REGENERATION

To borrow a phrase from the Old Testament prophet Amos, those who are at ease in Zion are the primary villains to the Western writers of the Gilded Age. Perhaps this, as well as any single factor, explains the cultural miasma which hangs over the writing of the period dealing not directly with the frontier but with the "agricultural paradise" succeeding it. From E.W. Howe's *The Story of a Country Town* through the works of Hamlin Garland and Sinclair Lewis to the present, the basic enemy in writing about rural America has been complacency, and the ultimate literary sin, unwillingness to change a bad present situation for an unknown future which, although it may not turn out better, will at least be different. This itself indicates, if only inversely, the general cultural importance of the idea of the frontier.

As a case in point let us briefly glance at how often in Hamlin Garland's *Main-Travelled Roads* the ideal of successful fulfillment in life is coupled with some image of escape from a stagnant rural society in which existence has turned sour. Howard McClane of "Up the Coule" is the most familiar example, but other less well-known characters also emphasize the idea that rural life, unmixed with any ideal of westering, is closer to hell on earth than to the heaven its proponents claim. In "Among the Corn Rows" a representative of the frontier, or at least of a society closer to it, rescues an almost legendary damsel in distress from the toils of a life not only of grinding poverty but of smug self-satisfaction. When Bob carries Julia off farther West, his action signifies not so much a change of geographical locale as a moral rebirth. Similarly, in "A Branch Road" Will is also able to rescue his bride only after some time spent working on the railroad, a clear image for the notion that going somewhere is what is important. Even Mrs. Ripley must leave, if only temporarily, the familiar routine she has endured all her life. In all these examples, the idea of the frontier plays an important metaphorical role.

[Historian] E.W. Howe's country town, left behind when the frontier passed it by and hence a stagnant backwater rather than a vibrant community, offers another striking image for essentially the same concern. The beginning line of Howe's tale, "Ours was the prairie district, out West, where we had gone to grow up with the country," is immediately qualified by the notation that "our section was not a favorite" and that other settlers went farther West. It is not beside the point to note as well that the town is named Fairview, another hint that the going may be better if one moves on.

HOWELLS AND THE CITY AS A FRONTIER

When William Dean Howells, in consonance with Horace Greeley's practice rather than his precept, left Ohio for the East, he was in his own person expressing the validity of frontier mythology, even though his removal to Boston and later to New York is often interpreted as a denial of his Western heritage. The opposite point, that Howells by his move East and subsequent admission to the Eastern literary establishment was affirming rather than denying frontier values, seems more valid. Howells is a good figure with whom to close this discussion because his career as a man of letters sums up, better than any of his contemporaries', the ideals of the new start symbolized by the presence of the frontier. Born a poor Ohio boy, at his death Howells was the preeminent man of letters in the United States, and his career indicated to many of his fellow Americans the nearly limitless opportunities available to one who, primarily by hard work, was willing to wrest success from the unpromising intellectual landscape of the United States just as his more muscular countrymen had wrested it from the often unpromising physical environment of the West.

Howells was, his contemporaries would instantly have noted, a writer of utopias. *A Traveller from Altruria*, although by no means so popular as *Looking Backward*, was still one of the best sellers of the late nineteenth century. Like the latter, it too is interpretable as a statement of the primacy of frontier values, insofar as Howells's *Traveller* castigates Gilded Age society on the basis of values to be found in another country, albeit one which is not specifically located across the wide Missouri. The promises of Altruria are basically those offered by the frontier and are attainable by those willing to seek them out.

A Hazard of New Fortunes is similar, although here the story is much more directly related to Howells's own biography. In this novel Howells took the chance to show his public that he would practice what he preached. It becomes clear during the course of the novel that the gain was worth the risk involved. Life in New York rejuvenates March, just as it had revitalized Howells. March has accepted the challenge of the frontier, realizing that refusal to adapt is only another term for moral cowardice.

In closing let us mention an oft-noted point about Howells—his championing of new American literary talent, much of it Western. A close friend of Mark Twain (his essay "My Mark Twain" remains one of the best appreciations of that author), he also championed Hamlin Garland when that very different young Western author was trying to get a start. The fictional worlds of both authors are vastly different from Howells's own as well as from each other's; but to deny either one would have been to deny a major premise on which Howells had built his life and around which he organized his fiction: the premise of that constant renewal necessary for literature, symbolized by the frontier.

The Small Town in American Realism

Anthony Channell Hilfer

America has always idealized the small town and
small town life. The more America modernizes and
changes, the more American culture tends to yearn
for a return to the innocence and serenity of the
small town. Writers such as Sarah Orne Jewett and
even Hamlin Garland upheld small town values of
honesty, decency, and moral uprightness as the
more ruthless and combative values of the city
encroached. However, because the image of the
small town as a repository of socially nurturing
"traditional values" is something of an idealization,
Realist fiction has often attacked it. Mark Twain was
particularly contemptuous of the small towns along
the Mississippi River in *The Adventures of Huckleberry Finn*, and a lot of his later novels and short
stories attack the complacency and hypocrisy of
small town values. Negative commentary on the
narrowness and stifling conformity of the small town
continued into the early twentieth century in the
works of writers such as Edgar Lee Masters, Sherwood Anderson, Thomas Wolfe, and Sinclair Lewis.
As a result, a strand of Realism, which has come to
be known as "The Revolt from the Village," has established itself in American literature. Anthony Hilfer
has also written *American Fiction Since 1940* (1992),
and *The Crime Novel: A Deviant Genre* (1990).

[Poet and critic] Carl Van Doren identified "The Revolt from
the Village" in 1921 in one of a series of articles on contemporary American fiction which he wrote for the *Nation*. Certain American novelists, Van Doren announced, were attacking one of the most cherished American beliefs: the belief

that the American small town is a place characterized by sweet innocence, an environment in which the best in human nature could flower serenely, a rural paradise exempt from the vices, complexities, and irremediable tragedies of the city. These American writers were presenting a quite different and more realistic interpretation of the town, emphasizing its moral repressiveness and stultifying conformity, and protesting its standardized dullness. The protest began with *Spoon River Anthology* in 1915 and continued in *Winesburg, Ohio* (1919) but its *annus mirabilis* was 1920 with the publication of *Main Street*, which led what had become a full-scale assault. . . .

The authors drew on the real towns of their childhood, but their creations are fictions, simpler and more patterned than any reality. What they opposed was not an actual village existing in time and space but a mental conception of the village existing in the mind of a great number of Americans.

THE MYTH OF THE AMERICAN TOWN

The village was synechdoche and metaphor. The village represented what Americans thought they were, what they sometimes pretended (to themselves as well as others) they wanted to be, and if the small town was typically American, the Midwestern small town was doubly typical. The basic civilization of America was middle class, a fact somewhat obscured in city novels that tended to treat the extremes of the very rich and the very poor to the exclusion of the middle. Even the East, dominated by its cities, usually granted the superior "Americanism" of the Middle West. Thus the Midwestern novelists of the teens and twenties could see their locale as a microcosm of the nation and, provincial bourgeoises that they were, of the world. But their view was critical. The town was the focus of what was in actuality an over-all attack on middle-class American civilization.

The town was especially vulnerable because it had been mythicized out of all reality. The myth of the small town was based on a set of ideal antitheses to the city. The cold impersonality of the city contrasted with the "togetherness" of the town; the vice of the city with the innocence of the town; the complexity of the city with the simplicity of the town. The sociological cause of the myth is evident enough: the myth of the small town served as a mental escape from the complexities, insecurities, and continual changes of a society in rapid transition from a dominantly rural to a dominantly urban and industrial civilization. The myth was a symptom of immaturity; it was sentimental, escapist, and simple-minded. . . .

The small town myth . . . is primarily a myth of community. If some of the classic American writers such as Hawthorne, Melville, Twain, and James tried to create through the verbal structures of their fiction an ideal community, "a world elsewhere," those who glorified the American village community complacently assured their readers that the ideal community really existed: it was the American small town. Because the town myth appeals so strongly to the American desire for community, it has been much more important to American literature than the agrarian myth. . . .

The small town, it is true, equally lacks glamour, but its very freedom from glamour and excitement was one of its endearing qualities to the American consciousness, and it has never lacked a literature of glorification. . . .

SARAH ORNE JEWETT'S CELEBRATION OF THE SMALL TOWN

The Country of the Pointed Firs (1896), [Sarah Orne] Jewett's account of Dunnet Landing, a seacoast village in Maine, is neither sentimental nor unrealistic. The stories are accurate, sometimes brilliant vignettes of a New England town that is well past its economic and social prime. In one of Miss Jewett's stories, a character comments on the growing provincialism and narrowness of the community since the decline of shipping; in another story, Miss Jewett notes a country graveyard in which most of the home graves are those of women—the men having died in the war or at sea or gone west. The decline of New England into an increasingly marginal area is acknowledged if not emphasized in these stories. . . .

The narrator comes to Dunnet Landing as an escape from the city that threatens her sense of identity and coherence:

> The hurry of life in a large town, the constant putting aside of preference to yield to a most unsatisfactory activity, began to vex me, and one day I took the train, and only left it for the eastward bound boat. Carlyle says somewhere that the only happiness a man ought to ask for is happiness enough to get his work done; and against this the complexity and futile ingenuity of social life seems a conspiracy. But the first salt wind from the east, the first sight of a lighthouse set boldly on its outer rock, the flash of a gull, the waiting procession of

seaward-bound firs on an island made me feel solid and definite again, instead of a poor incoherent being.

This quotation illustrates the positive values of the isolated village as an escape from the futile dissipation of self that seems a condition of urban living. But only a few sentences later the narrator describes the coast as "cold and sterile"; the escape has its costs. . . .

The small town, as Miss Jewett sees it, is closer to the private island than to the city. The town is an escape from the complications and emotional demands of the city, its distractions and artifices into a place of peace where private memories whether of joy or more often of grief can be clearly and simply defined and then hung onto as a basis for life. . . . Things *have* happened in Dunnet Landing, but it is the past happenings and relationships that sustain the characters. Nothing *does* happen in Miss Jewett's stories because the stories and their setting are an escape, not only from the distraction and confusion of life, but also from its immediacy and intensity. The escape from complication is, in truth, an escape from the less manageable forms of life itself.

THORNTON WILDER'S REPRESENTATIVE AMERICAN TOWN

Thornton Wilder's *Our Town* (1938) resembles Miss Jewett's work in its image of a New England town as a pastoral retreat. Wilder's town, however, is more mythological and far less tied to reality than is Miss Jewett's. Grover's Corners, population 2,640, is described as a "very ordinary town." A bit dull, the audience is told, but the young people seem to like it since 90 per cent of those graduating from high school settle down there. These mythical statistics are attributed to a New England town of the 1900–10 period, a time of actual widespread exodus from New England farms and small towns to larger towns and cities. Another strange thing about Grover's Corners is the Spartan quality of its middle-class wives, such as those the Stage Manager eulogizes. "I don't have to point out to the women in my audience that those ladies they see before them, both these ladies cooked three meals a day,—one of 'em for twenty years, the other for forty,—and no summer vacation. They brought up two children a piece; washed; cleaned the house—and never a nervous breakdown. Never thought themselves hard used either." Earlier in the play the Stage Manager has told us of "Polish town" across the tracks.

These New England ladies, unlike those in the rest of the country, take no advantage of this abundant supply of cheap maid service. Moreover, they suffer none of the breakdowns and show none of the queerness that native New England authors like Mary Wilkins described at about the same period in which Wilder's play is set.

Wilder's play could hardly afford to be realistic on these points. To have indicated the actual exodus from the New England small town would have subverted the smug complacency of the play's presentation of Grover's Corners as the great good place. Similarly out of place would have been a depiction of the actual queerness and meanness of small-town New England. For Grover's Corners does not represent an actual New Hampshire village but yet another version of the earthly paradise where life is simple, "natural," and "real." To emphasize their reality, Wilder has his characters speak entirely in clichés. The use of cliché is not, of course, the result of lack of sophistication or skill on Wilder's part. The clichés are deliberately calculated, and we are meant to see eternal truths behind them, truths all the more valid and universal because of their unpretentiously hackneyed form of expression. The action of the play is also a series of clichés, again quite calculated. As the Stage Manager sums it up: "The First Act was called the Daily Life. This Act is called Love and Marriage. There's another act coming after this: I reckon you can guess what that's about."

Life seen from this perspective is itself a mellow cliché, holding no surprises, no terrors, Wilder uses the Stage Manager to enforce this perspective. From the Stage Manager's point of view, everything has already happened; events are robbed of their shock power and reduced to illustrations of the typical, the typical itself being defined in comfortably conventional middle-class terms. The knowledge that everything that happens is *natural,* and therefore good, is soothing. Even death has no sting in *Our Town* since, as the Stage Manager assures us, "There's something way down deep that's eternal about every human being."

Despite Wilder's knowing way with clichés, his play is, in fact, genuinely banal in its conception, and its language is smugly unpretentious and non-intellectual. Miss Jewett created a personal refuge out of real materials; Wilder merely mirrors the refuge of the collective American psyche: a simplified and idealized small town, a not too spacious womb in which the realities of time, history, and death can be evaded. . . .

DREISER'S REJECTION OF THE TOWN FOR THE CITY

To Dreiser, the town and farm emotionally represented the charm and appeal of childhood, but it was an appeal the adult had to resist. The city, by contrast, represented the appalling but *vital* present. The polarization is especially clear in an illuminating passage from *Newspaper Days* in which Dreiser recounts his visit to the Missouri farm of his fiancée's parents:

> To me it seemed that all the spirit of rural America, its idealism, its dreams, the passions of a [John] Brown, the courage and patience and sadness of a Lincoln, the dreams and courage of a Lee or Jackson, all were here. The very soil smacked of American idealism and faith, a fixedness in sentimental and purely imaginative American tradition, in which I, alas! could not share. I was enraptured. Out of its charms and sentiments I might have composed an elegy or an epic, but I could not believe that it was more than a frail flower of romance. I had seen Pittsburgh. . . . I had seen Lithuanians and Hungarians in their "courts and hovels," I had seen the girls of that city walking the streets at night. This profound faith in God, in goodness, in virtue and duty that I saw here in no wise squared with the craft, the cruelty, the brutality and envy that I saw everywhere else. These parents were gracious and God-fearing, but to me they seemed asleep. They did not know life—could not. These boys and girls, as I soon found, respected love and marriage and duty and other things which the idealistic American still clings to.
>
> Outside was all this other life that I had seen of which apparently these people knew nothing. They were as if suspended in dreams, lotus eaters.

Dreiser's own writings show his freedom from the obsolete dreams of the farm and village. Indeed, the condition of a healthy American literature was to reject and destroy the myth of the village, for the whole myth was based on conceptions profoundly hostile to the imagination. The myth denied satire, tragedy, even comedy. Many small-town novels operating within the myth do attempt comedy but it is ersatz comedy, the kind that is supposed to prompt a gentle chuckle at the lovable foolishness of various good-hearted eccentrics. The archetypal subject of most genuine comedy—sex—is conspicuous by its absence. Satire would, of course, have spilled the beans, exposing all the illusions and lies that the myth was meant to promote—especially the illusion of middle-class virtue. Finally, the mythical village was anti-tragic. People could die there but never alone, never meaninglessly. Moreover, fiction written within the myth accepted a prescribed bourgeois morality. This does not mean that it was self-righteously puritanical. A "ruined" girl might be a sympathetic character, for instance, *but* only if she were properly repentant and properly unhappy about it. Dreiser's own *Sister Carrie* upset people because, although its heroine was unhappy at the end of the novel, it was not because she had "sinned"; *that* did not bother her or Dreiser either.

DREISER'S IMPORTANCE

Dreiser was a central influence in the revolt from the village though he himself found his themes in the city or the industrial town. Dreiser's main contributions were two: first, he began the breakthrough to an honest treatment of sex; second, he developed the emotional mode of naturalistic pathos, a mode that defined his world in tragic rather than ethical terms, the tragic *emotion* of pity being substituted for an ethical *judgment*. Dreiser freed writers to treat American life with honest and genuine, rather than faked, pathos. Dreiser's naturalism has been often maligned for supposedly reducing human dignity. In theory, this is true. In practice, the small-town myth that never questioned genteel ideals denied the dignity of suffering by false optimistic assurances or sentimentalized pieties. Pathos never really *counted;* it was used sentimentally, purely for the momentary sensation. Naturalistic pathos, by contrast, is final; there is no happy end.

Naturalistic pathos is mostly to be found in Masters, Anderson, and Wolfe, all of whom gave new dimensions to the theme of "the buried life.". . .

CONFORMITY AND THE "BURIED LIFE"

To American writers, it seemed as though their civilization—puritanical and materialistic—stultified life by denying, suppressing, and repressing the buried life, particularly in its most charged and painful burden of sexual feeling. To blame the puritans was, of course, too simple. Introspection was really part of, rather than opposed to, the puritan tradition. The enemy was a decayed form of puritanism, more aptly termed Victorianism or the genteel tradition. This puritanism (for convenience I shall follow the historically over-simplified usage of the teens and twenties in referring to all phenomena of sexual prudery and repression as puritanism) shrank from the inner life, burying it under the restraints of shame and ignorance. Despite his historical errors, the most interesting analysis of the buried life is that of Van Wyck Brooks, who put in abstract terms the ideas that Masters and Anderson embodied in literary forms.

But Brooks is important not so much because of his considerable influence but because he was the popularizer, summarizer, and symbolic representative of the theme of the buried life. Other writers may have had earlier and perhaps even more intelligent insights into the buried life than did Brooks, but no one so completely and consistently pursued and identified himself with the theme. In just such a way is H.L. Mencken the representative of the attack on conformity, on the stereotyped thoughts and values of the herd mind. Writing in the Menckenian tradition, Sinclair Lewis and T.S. Stribling tended toward sociological fiction that assaulted the values and standards of the dominant middle class. A rough distinction between these two groups of writers is that the delineators of the buried life were concerned with hidden, misunderstood, inarticulate *feelings*, whereas the anticonformists were bothered by failures and suppressions of *thought*. Most Americans, the anticonformists believed, were incapable of genuine thought and distrusted and punished the few genuine thinkers in their midst. Placing themselves apart from the culture as though they were anthropologists observing some primitive tribe, Mencken, Lewis, and Stribling analyzed the strange mores and rituals of the *homo Americanus*. The result, however, was not sociological observation but a satire that used sociology as a convenient weapon.

The two themes of the buried life and the attack on conformity *are* the revolt from the village. H.L. Mencken was quite correct in his belief that the creative outburst of the teens and twenties was not a concerted movement but a case of each writer's responding individually. What gave the revolt unity was that a number of writers, drawing from quite varied sources and influences, arrived at common themes. Even the difference between the two major groups is a matter of emphasis. Mencken and Lewis wrote (badly) about the buried life; Brooks and Anderson attacked American conformity. Although both themes go well beyond the small town in scope, both focus on the town. The town was, of course, what many of these writers knew, what came to hand, and even for such Eastern urbanites as Brooks and Mencken, the town was nicely adaptable to serving as an image for their major themes. To show the buried life of a town was, implicitly, to deny that a refuge could be found from the fear, loneliness, and insecurity of an urbanizing society. These alien and disorienting emotions had to be recognized and faced; American literature offered a mirror image of them, no longer an escape from them. The necessary refuge had to be found in creative acts of the spirit rather than in sentimental falsifications of reality. One of these creative acts was to honor and celebrate rather than evade the pathos of a lonely society.

SMALL TOWN ANTI-INTELLECTUALISM

The anticonformists had equal reason to concentrate on the town. Most Americans recognized a certain lack of depth, originality, and variety in the small-town intellect, but most Americans demonstrated a definite fear of intellect as well. Glorification of the small town was one of the many proofs of how unnecessary intellect was as opposed to "horse sense," simple honesty, etc. This function of the small-town myth shows most clearly in its use by business and the Republican party even though, ironically, it was the dynamics of business that was turning America into an urban and industrial nation. But whenever the immense problems, the needs for centralized control and increased governmental responsibility that these new conditions created were cited, the business propaganda mill would respond with question-begging evocations of a vanished (indeed, never-existent), idyllic, individualistic, small-town civilization wherein such controls were entirely unnecessary. To problems of urban crime and chaos, the propaganda responded by a self-righteous recommendation of small-town virtues, virtues that the small town doubtfully possessed and that were thoroughly inappropriate to national problems. Praise of the small town was a covert way of denying the need to think, a method of evading the admission that old formulas no longer served the new conditions.

THE PROBLEM OF THE TOWN IN AMERICAN REALISM

The small towns of the myth were more virtuous and less complicated than any real small town, but the small towns of the new fiction were not entirely real either. In opposition to the idealized village of the myth, the rebels opposed an equally partial image made up of all the things that had been left out—the conformity, stupidity, loneliness, meanness, and physical ugliness of the village. They attacked an abstraction with a counter-abstraction. Yet of the two pictures, that of the rebels is far truer, for their abstractions were employed as a method rather than an evasion of thought and feeling. The harshness of their picture seems extreme only when we forget the ever-present tendency in American civilization to deny the bleaker realities.

The Rise of the City in American Realism

Sidney H. Bremer

More than any other phenomenon, the rise of the
modern city—and the social and economic tensions
these new urban spaces engendered—seemed to
epitomize the Age of Realism. The Realists' engagement with the rise of the city is reflected in the fiction of writers as diverse as William Dean Howells,
Edith Wharton, Stephen Crane, and Frank Norris.
Reformers and journalists such as Upton Sinclair
and Jacob Riis also exposed the horrendous living
conditions of the urban, immigrant poor. Often the
city was seen as a vast, incomprehensible machine,
while other writers portrayed it as a kind of modern
jungle, where primitive struggles for power and
dominance were played out. The rise of the city also
introduced conditions now accepted as part of modern living: the decline of rural communities, individual isolation and alienation, and the degradation of
the natural environment. The Realists fully confronted the consequences of urban growth, and Sidney Bremer illustrates the range and complexity of
their responses to the idea of the city. Bremer sees
Chicago as the representative late nineteenth century
American city, with its explosive growth, its ethnic
diversity, and its obsession with wealth and power.
Sidney Bremer has for many years taught Women's
Studies and American Studies at the University of
Wisconsin at Green Bay.

After the Civil War, the abstract city [in popular imagination]
called for exemplification. U.S. authors began to introduce
cities as national centers. Among major cities in the latter
half of the nineteenth century, however, Philadelphia proved

Excerpted from *Urban Intersections: Meetings of Life and Literature in United States Cities*, by Sidney H. Bremer. Copyright ©1992 by the Board of Trustees of the University of Illinois. Used with permission of the University of Illinois Press.

too old, Washington too merely political, Boston too merely cultural, and New York not sufficiently industrial to sustain symbolic status as *the* American city. *Waiting for the Verdict* (1867) by Rebecca Harding Davis, *Democracy* (1880) by Henry Adams, and *The Bostonians* (1886) by Henry James— while concerning themselves primarily with social caste, political power, and cultural reform—dramatize the respective inadequacies of Philadelphia, Washington, and Boston as national cities. None has held a prominent place in national literary imagery since then. As an alternative to cultural Boston, commercial New York seemed more promising at first—in *The Bostonians,* then in the work of William Dean Howells. Indeed "the Dean of American letters" contrasted the old city-town and the new economic city with almost schematic precision in *The Rise of Silas Lapham* (1885) and *A Hazard of New Fortunes* (1890). But even though New York City has figured prominently in our imaginative literature from Washington Irving to Grace Paley, *A Hazard of New Fortunes* set the stage for Chicago, not New York, to gain the title of national city. It was Chicago, a new industrial city, that proved most compelling for a nation using technology to reunite after civil war. New York would have to wait to take center stage as a cosmopolitan world city after the First World War. . . .

HOWELLS'S BOSTON AND NEW YORK NOVELS

The eclipse of regional Boston by the large-scale public economy of New York becomes clear in the pointed contrasts between *The Rise of Silas Lapham* and *A Hazard of New Fortunes.* Despite omens of the rising economic city, Howells's Boston centers on a homogeneous, largely private society of well-born families, mercantile gentility, and cultural refinement. His New York emerges as a heterogeneous, public society shaped by economic interests and mechanical transit networks. Just five years, yet worlds of difference, separate the two urban novels.

"Money is to the fore now. It is the romance, the poetry of our age," laments Bromfield Corey, the male representative of refined Boston in *The Rise of Silas Lapham.* His statement identifies the primacy of economic forces in the postwar nation, invading even Boston. The self-conscious aging of Bromfield Corey, whose inherited fortune derives from colonial sea trade, and his son Tom's decision to work for Silas

Lapham's paint manufacturing company signal Howells's recognition that the nation's urban economy was shifting from a mercantile to an industrial base. Within this context, Howells introduces the entrepreneur as the characteristic "type of the successful American," for so Silas Lapham seems through the public clichés of a newspaper interview. His credentials are money, not family membership in society, and his move to Boston from Vermont enacts the Horatio Alger myth of urban opportunity. . . .

It is hard to resist the idea that Howells created A *Hazard of New Fortunes* as a counterpoint to his Bostonian parable of individual moral success. Certainly his first New York novel offers analogous metaphors and key incidents. In place of Boston's private family homes, New York offers apartments, rented rooms, and a commercial "house." Part I is organized around the hunt for a New York apartment by the primary observers of the novel's events, Basil and Isabel March from Boston. Basil declares that the typical New York "flat abolishes the family consciousness" while it gives "artificial people a society basis on a little money." No one lives in a private home; several characters live in a boarding house that one runs, and another sets up his quarters over the offices of the magazine, the "house" that brings them all together. Not the family but money underlies the structure of this city. . . .

The shift proved as uncomfortable for others as for Howells. Authors otherwise radically different from each other, like Dreiser and Wharton, dramatized alienation—from others and from self—as a consequence of confronting the city as an external phenomenon. The economic city broke down continuities in the human "life-world," obscuring and thus diverting human beings' expressive connections to the city's social, physical, and cultural environment. Lost was the collective psychological power that the city-town fostered by maintaining a sense of continuity and community. . . .

The economic city in U.S. literature ascended to represent "the city" in mainstream consciousness, while women and ethnic minority and regional writers quietly continued to explore those common urban experiences that did not fit with the alienation of middle-class mobile white male writers like Howells. It is here that urban literary imagery divides, and no better example of this can be found than in turn-of-the-century Chicago literature. . . .

THE RISE OF CHICAGO

Chicago remained the nation's representative city long past the [1893] world's fair not because it was seen as average but because it was promoted as an epitome. The publicity surrounding the fair established the grounds on which writers built. Following the lead of Howells's *A Hazard of New Fortunes,* Chicago was presented as a city of national interest by mostly male writers, often from other parts of the country, and now best known for their Chicago novels: most famously Theodore Dreiser's *Sister Carrie* (1900) and *The Titan* (1914), *The Pit* (1903) by Frank Norris, and *The Jungle* (1906) by Upton Sinclair; from local pens, Henry Blake Fuller's *The Cliff-Dwellers* (1893) and *With the Procession* (1895) as well as Robert Herrick's *Memoirs of an American Citizen* (1905) and other Chicago novels. Hamlin Garland's *Rose of Dutcher's Coolly* (1895) and Willa Cather's *The Song of the Lark* (1915), by authors best known for other Midwest writing, also remain available to readers, as does Frank Harris's minor work, *The Bomb* (1908). . . .

SISTER CARRIE AND CHICAGO

Theodore Dreiser's *Sister Carrie* is only the best and most famous literary testament to the "many and growing commercial opportunities" that helped to make Chicago "a giant magnet" for Carrie Meeber's real-life counterparts, including novelists. *Sister Carrie* warms up to its Chicago theme more gradually, but no less deliberately than most. By quietly contrasting the "small . . . cheap . . . small . . . scrap" of Carrie's resources and "the great city" toward which she travels, Dreiser's opening paragraphs point toward Chicago as a threatening phenomenon. The novel then builds metaphoric intensity by generalizing about "the city" as a "superhuman" seducer and by prefiguring Chicago in the person of Charlie Drouet—both a commercial "drummer" for Chicago's goods and an amoral "masher" like Chicago itself. After Carrie gathers her first disoriented impressions of the city itself, Dreiser abruptly interrupts the plot line: "Before following her in her round of [job] seeking, let us look at the sphere in which her future was to lie." Several pages of exposition follow this self-conscious break. Emphasizing Chicago's "magnetic" power to attract new adherents and thus to expand itself, Dreiser links his metaphor of superhuman seduction to

a detailed mapping of the city's "vast wholesale and shop-
ping district.". . .

INDIVIDUALISM AND THE CITY

Lone newcomers figure as the main characters in most standard Chicago novels. Even when they arrive with other family members, most soon find themselves on their own—like
runaway Carrie Meeber. Thus translating the general statistical growth in Chicago's population into individuals' separate encounters with the city, the novels present an atomized
image of Chicago's new inhabitants. Unlike the immigrants

THE BEAUTY AND HORROR OF CHICAGO

This excerpt from Frank Norris's 1903 novel The Pit *conveys the energy and economic significance of Chicago,
which both fascinates and horrifies the central character, Laura
Dearborn.*

Chicago, the great grey city, interested her at every instant and
under every condition. As yet she was not sure that she liked it;
she could not forgive its dirty streets, the unspeakable squalor of
some of its poorer neighbourhoods that sometimes developed,
like cancerous growths, in the very heart of fine residence districts. The black murk that closed every vista of the business
streets oppressed her, and the soot that stained linen and gloves
each time she stirred abroad was a never-ending distress.

But the life was tremendous. All around, on every side, in
every direction the vast machinery of Commonwealth clashed
and thundered from dawn to dark and from dark till dawn.
Even now, as the car carried her farther into the business
quarter, she could hear it, see it, and feel in her every fibre the
trepidation of its motion. . . .

Suddenly the meaning and significance of it all dawned
upon Laura. The Great Grey City, brooking no rival, imposed
its dominion upon a reach of country larger than many a king-
dom of the Old World. For thousands of miles beyond its confines was its influence felt. Out, far out, far away in the snow
and shadow of northern Wisconsin forests, axes and saws bit
the bark of century-old trees, stimulated by this city's energy.
Just as far to the southward pick and drill leaped to the assault
of veins of anthracite, moved by her central power. Her force
turned the wheels of harvester and seeder a thousand miles
distant in Iowa and Kansas. Her force spun the screws and
propellers of innumerable squadrons of lake steamers crowd-

who in fact swelled Chicago's population, in fiction most of Chicago's new arrivals come from small U.S. towns. They share the national values and beliefs associated with individualism, yet their stories dramatize the impossibility for even acculturated Americans to manage Chicago's massing energies. As the typical newcomer approaches Chicago by train, the city's "enormous" power and "perplexing" mystery evoke utter confusion, deepening the danger of being thrown upon one's own resources, as these characters inevitably are, within the city. . . .

Such fictional Chicagoans form no sustaining allegiances,

---

ing the Sault Sainte Marie. For her and because of her all the Central States, all the great Northwest roared with traffic and industry; sawmills screamed; factories, their smoke blackening the sky, clashed and flamed; wheels turned, pistons leaped in their cylinders; cog gripped cog; beltings clasped the drums of mammoth wheels; and converters of forges belched into the clouded air their tempest breath of molten steel.

It was Empire, the resistless subjugation of all this central world of the lakes and the prairies. Here, midmost in the land, beat the Heart of the Nation, whence inevitably must come its immeasurable power, its infinite, infinite, inexhaustible vitality. Here, of all her cities, throbbed the true life—the true power and spirit of America; gigantic, crude with the crudity of youth, disdaining rivalry; sane and healthy and vigorous; brutal in its ambition, arrogant in the new-found knowledge of its giant strength, prodigal of its wealth, infinite in its desires. In its capacity boundless, in its courage indomitable; subduing the wilderness in a single generation, defying calamity, and through the flame and the débris of a commonwealth in ashes, rising suddenly renewed, formidable, and Titanic.

Laura, her eyes dizzied, her ears stunned, watched tirelessly. "There is something terrible about it," she murmured, half to herself, "something insensate. In a way, it doesn't seem human. It's like a great tidal wave. It's all very well for the individual just so long as he can keep afloat, but once fallen, how horribly quick it would crush him, annihilate him, how horribly quick, and with such horrible indifference! I suppose it's civilisation in the making, the thing that isn't meant to be seen, as though it were too elemental, too—primordial; like the first verses of Genesis."

Reprinted from Frank Norris, *The Pit: A Story of Chicago* (New York: Penguin 1994), pp. 55–58.

just temporary alliances. With only personal ambition to guide her, a Chicago newcomer like Dreiser's Sister Carrie moves all too easily and alone from one sector of urban society to another, "a Waif amid Forces" of wealth and poverty. Carrie cuts off all contact with her family when she moves out of her sister's flat and into Charlie Drouet's, and she loses touch, in turn, with Charlie and his successor, George Hurstwood, as she moves economically upward, finally into the more closely knit "Walled City" of New York. She even changes her name as she goes. The multiple roles taken on in Chicago by Sister Carrie—alias Carrie Meeber, alias Mrs. Drouet, alias Mrs. Wheeler, alias Carrie Madenda—are neither bent toward nor supported by any social community. As a result, she has no continuing identity. And her unnamed yet poignant dissatisfaction, as she repeatedly sits in rocking chairs at windows, alone and disconnected from the city she overlooks, reflects psychic dissociation as the ultimate cost of such individualism. Relying only on herself, Carrie becomes separated from herself. Individualism threatens psychological alienation as well as social collapse in this and other standard Chicago novels.

Reckless individualism is also embodied in Chicago's built environment in these novels. Skyscrapers flaunt individual ambition, while streetcar monopolies deepen social divisions by oppressing labor and segregating residential districts. The upwardly and outwardly expanding structures induce psychological distress. Skyscrapers and streetcar lines create a sense of powerlessness. Their enormity dwarfs ordinary people, despite being manifestations of humankind's soaring imagination and technological know-how. Their physical extension is unsettling, pointing toward a future of "indefinite continuation," of constant expansion "in anticipation of rapid growth." Most importantly, they seem to defy natural laws without expressing any alternative, communal order. . . .

GREED, SPECULATION, AND HIGH FINANCE

Standard Chicago novels devote so much attention to documenting the details of finance that they often read like business primers. Such documentation asserts the centricity of economic individualism and the economic machinery it masks in Chicago. The novels do not demystify the economic base of the city in exposing its power and destructive effects, however. Instead they further its mythic dominance by personifying it in the tycoon, weighting him with all their exclamatory and explanatory rhetoric, and embedding his story in their contrasting structures. Only Herrick's *The Memoirs of an American Citizen* exhibits baldly—without elaborate commentary—the emptiness of the tycoon's identification with the city environment and the demoralizing impact of his material grandiosity and Chicago's upon the entire nation's civic life. *The Pit* is far more typical in raising the voice of the standard Chicago novel to its "epic" pitch. Using monopolistic capitalism as a vainglorious assertion of individualism, "Napoleonic" Curtis Jadwin's dealings on the Chicago Board of Trade unleash a "mighty" and unnatural whirlpool that swirls "far out through the city's channels" to move "grain in the elevators of Western Iowa" and carry "men upon the streets of New York . . . bewildered and unresisting back and downward into the Pit itself." Its "undertow" leaves Jadwin himself financially and psychologically ruined. "I corner the wheat!" he finally explodes. "Great heavens, it is the wheat that has cornered me!" The city machine runs the rugged individual, not vice versa.

THE JUNGLE AND CHICAGO'S POOR

The perverse domination of Chicago by economic machinery is clearest, however, when Upton Sinclair turns attention to the poor. *The Jungle* differs from other standard Chicago novels in its focus on an immigrant and his family rather than on a lone Anglo-American. Its setting in Chicago's outlying slums and factories rather than in its railroading, skyscraping center and its dramatization of a struggle for survival rather than a battle for success also set it apart. Although nearly all the residential novels articulate grounds for communal life in Chicago, only *The Web of Life* and *The Common Lot* among standard Chicago novels share this focus with *The Jungle,* Sinclair's depiction of Chicago as the great and awful, national economic city prevents his work from breaking away from a divisive, dehumanizing portrayal. First alienated as a group by language and customs, Jurgis Rudkus's Lithuanian immigrant family is eventually broken apart by meat packers, realtors, criminals, and politicians. "Blind and insensate Greed" simultaneously separates and enslaves them all to a vast interlocking trust—a mechanized, monopolized version of Herrick's "web of petty greeds and blind efforts." Initially enthusiastic about becoming part of the slaughterhouse operation that efficiently turns sheep and hogs and cattle into canned meat and sausage and glue, Jurgis finds that he, like the animals, marches naively toward death. Weakened by overwork, he is discarded like the other "worn-out parts" of the great machine.

So strong is the Chicago belief in individual will, moreover, that Jurgis does not see himself as oppressed until his wife is raped and allowed to die along with his son, his sister-in-law becomes a prostitute and drug addict, and he and others are blackballed, jailed, and hospitalized by industrial forces. His eventual affirmation of the proletariat does not offer a clearly positive alternative, however; the collectivity he joins screams in the "voice of the wild beast, frantic, incoherent, maniacal." Indeed, that voice represents a politically logical but structurally discordant answer to the standard novels' questions about individualism. Like *The Web of Life, The Jungle* exemplifies critic Amy Kaplan's point that such wishful endings "embody the desire to posit an alternative reality" outside "the novel's construction of the real," namely, the economically divided and mechanized city. In fact, *The Jungle's* socialist resolution exceeded the limits and energies of this Chicago novel genre. Although Sinclair's muckraking spurred legislative action on the Pure Food and Drug Act and the Beef Inspection Act in 1907, eight years elapsed before the publication of another major Chicago standard novel. Based then on research that Dreiser undertook at the Newberry Library, *The Titan* has a déjà vu effect.

CRITICISM OF THE CITY IN CHICAGO'S REALIST FICTION

No passive part of Chicago's ascendancy as a national city, the standard Chicago novels essay a powerful critique of the city's meaning for the nation. Their alienated characters, unnatural settings, and economically enslaving plots demonstrate that belief in the primacy of the individual both exacerbates the excesses of modern urban life and proves inadequate to control them. Thus individualism undermines cooperation in Chicago's fragmented society, precludes any limits on how far a skyscraper or factory might flaunt its builder's pride, and masks the self-propelling forces of the city's economy. Conversely, the individual is powerless to contend against Chicago's social "battle-field," "Tartarean" environment, and economic "machine." Despite their critique of individualism, however, the novels actually reflect and perpetuate alienation through their structures. Despite the skyscraper collection of characters in *The Cliff-Dwellers* and the collectivism at the end of *The Jungle*, the novels concern themselves primarily with the individual's oppositional relationship to the city. Despite Herrick's desire to affirm interdependency in *The Common Lot* and *The Web of Life*, his emphasis remains on "individual ethical initiative" in "direct opposition to" urban industrialis. In his "iceberg"-cold decision to become "a part of *them*," Herrick's fictional double Howard Sommers recalls his historical precursor William Dean Howells's determination to exchange Boston's comforts for New York's "homelessness."

Within a national economic paradigm, such Chicago novels envision the city as an alien, external phenomenon. Their documentary detailing maintains distance from that phenomenon, their mythic metaphors belittle common human powers, and their contrasts preclude any human joinings. They support the "outside expert" approach to urban problems—and to cities as problems—still common to social scientific studies and governmental interventions today, and so deeply implicated in maintaining the status quo. Caught up in the national Chicago-watching that divided black city from white, the standard Chicago novels ignore the communal and organic continuities that were also a part of Chicago's Story.

CHAPTER 5

Realism After 1914

American
Realism

American Realism in the Postmodern Age

David E. Shi

At the dawn of the twenty-first century, when the all-powerful media is increasingly responsible for representing what people see of the world and for how they see it, many writers and thinkers now question the notion that there is indeed an objective "reality" outside of the self. In this excerpt, David E. Shi responds to accusations that Realism's goal of imitating the "real world" both visually and in writing is false and misleading, and he strongly asserts Realism's continuing relevance. According to Shi, the ideas of the nineteenth-century Realists still fulfill a commonly shared need on the part of individuals to be connected to the larger spectacle of humanity and the shared experiences and significance of everyday living. This is why Realism outlasted twentieth-century Modernism, and why it will continue to a dominant literary form in the twenty-first century. David E. Shi is a professor of history and president of Furman University, South Carolina. He is the author of *The Simple Life: Plain Living and High Thinking in American Culture* (1984), and, with George Brown Tindall, *America: A Narrative History* (1996).

Realism has not fared well of late within the higher reaches of the academy and among prominent segments of the artistic community. Much of the fiction and art produced during the Gilded Age is as out of fashion as the hansom cab and hooped skirt. Today, it seems, the gaslit, brownstone world represented by William Dean Howells and [painter] John Sloan evokes the poignance of a bygone era. What was vivid and valid for its own day has become bland and antique a century later. Many realistic works of art and literature have lost the sheen of novelty and seem terribly outdated.

But there is more at work than changing cultural fashions. Since the end of World War II, realism and its accompanying ideology of liberal humanism have become objects of ferocious contempt. The horrifying revelations of the Holocaust, the looming threat of nuclear annihilation, and the banal priorities and conformist imperatives of a runaway consumer culture have led many avant-garde writers and artists to view contemporary society as a nightmare from which they are trying to escape. Modern American culture has supposedly become so suffocating and corrupting, so vacuous and idiotic, that it is no longer worthy of mimetic representation. In 1961, for instance, novelist Philip Roth noted how difficult it was "to understand, describe, and then make *credible* much of American reality. It stupefies, it sickens, it infuriates, and finally it is even a kind of embarrassment to one's own meager imagination." Many thoughtful Americans, he reported, were spurning the "grander social and political phenomena of our times" in order to "take the self as their subject": the "sheer fact of self, the vision of self as inviolate, powerful, and nervy, self as the only real thing in an unreal environment."

POSTMODERNISM'S ATTACK ON REALISM

More recently, a burgeoning group of critical theorists—structuralists, post-structuralists, deconstructionists—has assaulted the mimetic tradition from a different angle. Drawing upon an array of reality-defying philosophers—Kant, Nietzsche, Heidegger—and employing an arsenal of opaque jargon and ingenious utterances, they dismiss representational art as a "vulgar illusion" and a "naive subterfuge." In their view, "reality" is a linguistic construct rather than something outside the self. The arts, therefore, can never truly represent or imitate the "actual" world. At best they can only mimic the discourses which fabricate that world. Viewed from this perspective, the methods of conventional realism—visual curiosity, common-sense empiricism, and rational analysis—are utterly inadequate tools for the imaginative artist living in a "postmodern" age. As literary critic Sven Birkerts maintains, the representational imperative championed by Whitman and Howells is now impossible because "our common reality has gradually grown out of reach of the realist's instruments."

Still other "antirealists" argue that the godless world out-side the self is not so much elusive and absurd as it is illu-sory. As a consequence, the best works of art and fiction "de-construct" themselves. That is, they reveal their own inability to mirror reality. In his brilliantly playful story, "The Death of the Novel," Ronald Sukenick declares: "Reality doesn't exist, time doesn't exist, personality doesn't exist." Sukenick con-tends that a "post-realist" literature should not try to repli-cate the "insipid" and "unreal" activities of bourgeois society. The "subject" of art is no longer relevant. Postmodern art and literature should escape from the tyranny of appearances and generate their own reality rooted in the idiosyncratic self. . . . It is time, he asserts, to abandon the false hope of rep-resenting a public reality and cultivate an extreme subjectiv-ity that borders on the hermetic and impenetrable.

Novelist William H. Gass said much the same when he announced in 1970 that the postmodern writer must keep readers "kindly imprisoned in his language, [for] there is lit-erally nothing beyond." At its best this anarchic insistence that meaning exists only in the mind of the beholder, that it is something to be created rather than mirrored, opens up infinite possibilities for inventive brilliance and the unfet-tered expression of things private and inward. At its worst, however, such a purely aesthetic perspective leads to a des-iccated self-consciousness and cheerful nihilism detached from the human community. [Author] Flannery O'Connor had such a self-referential outlook in mind when she said that the borders of reality for radical modernists were the sides of their skulls.

Some champions of postmodern fabulism have become so zealous in their rejection of the mimetic tradition that they deny *any* legitimacy to realism as a mode of cultural ex-pression. They dismiss representational art as an aesthetic placebo for bourgeois philistines. Realism, claims critic Robert Scholes, is dead, or, at least, irrelevant. Those hope-lessly backward writers and artists who still embrace the mimetic fallacy are like "headless chickens unaware of the decapitating axe." Such harsh attacks have led some to ques-tion whether realism is worth studying even as an *historical* phenomenon. Literary historian George Levine asks: "Given the disrepute of realism and the exposure of representation [as a false idea], what could be the point in reconsidering their status once again?"

REALISM'S SURVIVAL IN THE TWENTIETH CENTURY

An answer to Levine's question must begin with an obvious correction: reports of the death of realism and reality are greatly exaggerated. Some observers understood this almost a century ago. "Realism," the literary critic Bliss Perry predicted in 1902, "has wrought itself too thoroughly into the picture of the modern world, it is too significant a movement, to allow any doubt as to the permanence of its influence." The realistic impulse has since demonstrated a remarkable perseverance. Today, even in the face of the chic piety that the very notion of representing reality is a "sham," many Americans still savor artistic renderings of the world "out there" beyond the self. Countless writers and artists continue to produce convincing and compelling representations of observed fact that provoke powerful, complicated emotions. They do so without being defensive or apologetic. . . .

Even more than their nineteenth-century predecessors, contemporary realists are diverse in outlook and application. Some, such as writer Tom Wolfe, seek to revive the fact-mongering documentary emphasis of nineteenth-century fiction. He practices and promotes "a highly detailed realism based on reporting, . . . a realism that would portray the individual in intimate and inextricable relation to the society around him." Others profess a new realism informed by the psychological emphases and formal innovations of modernism. As a result, they are more aware of the problematic nature of representing *what is there* than the Dreiser who blithely asserted that "truth is what is." They recognize that seeing is not exactly the same as knowing and that facts are not always unambiguous. Reality to them is not simply what exists; it is fluid and pluralistic, provisional and uncertain, culturally conditioned and filtered through individual perception. Suggestion thus becomes as important a skill as enumeration. Yet for all of their modern sophistication, contemporary realists sustain the essential mission undertaken by [realist writers and painters such as] Howells and Homer, Jewett and Wharton, Sullivan, Eakins, Henri, and Lippmann: to find an accessible language or form to represent the vital concerns and recognizable features of the everyday world. "Making reality real," as [novelist] Eudora Welty insists, "is art's responsibility."

Welty posits an essential truth that we are always in danger of forgetting amid the narcissistic cant of self-reflexive modernism: we cannot afford to abandon the larger social scene, nor can we ignore the aesthetic pleasures contained in unadorned fact. Despite the self-contradictory claim that everything is merely fictive and verbal, there is a redemptive public realm "out there." It is not simply a figment of the imagination nor a semantic construct. Our common phenomenal world is a fact of life deserving of respect and recognition. The urge to represent it seems essential to human nature. "Reality is not something I chose," the "New Realist" painter Philip Pearlstein noted in 1973, "but something I found myself in." The ideal of facing and expressing the facts of everyday life and social relations, however imperfect the process might be, persists in large part because of the quiet grandeur inherent in the close observation and faithful rendering of the figures, objects, and concerns outside the self. "All I'm trying to do," Pearlstein remarked, "is to see things as they are."

It is in this context that the nineteenth-century realists retain a vibrant significance. The realistic enterprise, born out of faith in the importance of the social world and nourished by the methods and prestige of empirical science, brought a radiant energy to thought and the arts during the nineteenth century. In the process it helped displace a flaccid idealism. "The illegitimate monopoly which the genteel tradition had established over what ought to be assumed and what ought to be hoped for has been broken down," reported the Harvard philosopher George Santayana in 1913. While using "facts" to assault the patrician elite's stranglehold over high culture, realists helped create a self-conscious American philosophy, literature, art, and architecture. As Saul Bellow has testified, "the development of realism in the nineteenth century is still the major event of modern literature."

Whatever their animating impulse—a simple fascination with the visual world or an unabashed love of life, a curiosity about others, a quest for documentary truth or a commitment to functional design, a pagan acceptance of things as they are or an impassioned protest against injustice—the realists sought to transmute the raw materials of life into works of palpable truth and enduring insight. By rendering the ordinary significant and the hidden visible, by refusing to offer easy consolations or to rest content with cheap ironies, they demonstrated the power of representation to sustain, assure, and enlarge us. The realists, wrote Henry James, provided the pleasure of recognition and the prod of self-examination. In the process they taught the hard but vital lesson that life is often antagonistic to desire and that most people are morally mixed.

THE NEED FOR REALISM IN ART, LITERATURE, AND LIFE

In this super-sophisticated postmodern age, the realism of fact spawned during the nineteenth century remains thoroughly unfashionable and fundamentally important. Some quite intelligent and discerning people still long for the sympathetic humanism and trustworthy satisfactions evident in old-fashioned realistic fiction and art. "One of the literary secrets of our time," confessed novelist Cynthia Ozick in 1987, "is that we miss the nineteenth-century novel. We miss it intensely, urgently," and long for "an excursion, however humanly universal, into [its] lost conventions."

Ozick's honest yearning for a humane realism suggests that an essential task of thought and the arts is to help people connect with others. By entering into the emotions, aspirations, and limitations of others, nineteenth-century realists manifested a rejuvenating passion for the strange spectacle of humanity. Although often fraught with class biases, overheated virility, and unknowing condescension, their democratic aesthetic reminded people that they are helplessly interdependent. It also appealed to the unrelenting infatuation people have with themselves, their entanglements with neighbors, and their jarring encounters with the larger society and its ephemera. The literary critic Ludwig Lewisohn recognized in 1921 that it was realism's basic respect for people that made it "so sanative an influence amid the heat, the turmoil, and the moral malignities of society. To it there are no outcasts; none are disinherited, none wholly guilty, none stale or discarded. Thus beauty and truth, art and humanity meet and are one."

Today realism retains its artistic appeal as the United States struggles to embody its ideal as a nation proud of its diversity and just in its social transactions. Painter Willard Midgette stressed in 1978, shortly before his death, that he strove in his art to help "the people looking at the picture to make contact with the people in the picture." He clung tenaciously to the belief that realistic representation possesses a peculiar ability to intensify and extend a sense of social communion. For this reason alone, the creation of an "aesthetic of the common" and a "beloved community" remains a beckoning goal. "The idea of a democratic culture that extends beyond the academy," literary critic Irving Howe observed in 1989, "is one that we cannot afford to surrender, not if we remain attached to the idea of a democratic politics."

The extraordinary resilience of realism as a mode of cultural expression attests to its inherent appeal. In reflecting upon the redemptive ardor of the realistic enterprise, novelist John Updike recently declared that "Howells's agenda remains our agenda: for the American writer to live in America and to mirror it in writing, with 'everything brought out.'" Updike then quoted a letter in which an elderly Howells told Charles Eliot Norton that he was "not sorry for having wrought in common, crude material so much; that is the right American stuff. . . . I was always, as I still am, trying to fashion a piece of literature out of the life next at hand." Updike's conclusion shimmers with conviction: "It is hard to see, more than eight decades later, what else can be done."

CHRONOLOGY

1859

Charles Darwin, *On the Origin of the Species.*

1865

Civil War ends with Lee's surrender at Appomattox; Lincoln is assassinated; the Thirteenth Amendment abolishes slavery; Mark Twain, "The Celebrated Jumping Frog of Calaveras County."

1867

First Reconstruction Act passed, aimed at rebuilding the South in the postslavery era.

1868

Fourteenth Amendment passes, guaranteeing civil rights; Bret Harte, *The Luck of Roaring Camp.*

1869

Ulysses S. Grant elected president for the first of two terms; Union Pacific–Central Pacific transcontinental railroad completed; Mark Twain, *The Innocents Abroad;* Bret Harte, *The Outcasts of Poker Flat.*

1870

Novelist Frank Norris born; John D. Rockefeller founds Standard Oil.

1871

Novelists Stephen Crane and Theodore Dreiser born.

1872

Mark Twain, *Roughing It.*

1873

Grant administration implicated in serious financial scandals; Andrew Carnegie's Bethlehem Steel Company begins production in Pittsburgh; Mark Twain and Charles Dudley Warner, *The Gilded Age.*

1876

Alexander Graham Bell invents the telephone; Henry James, *Rod-*

erick Hudson; Mark Twain, *The Adventures of Tom Sawyer;* novelists Sherwood Anderson, Willa Cather, and Jack London born.

1877

End of Reconstruction in the South; Henry James, *The American;* Thomas Edison invents the phonograph.

1878

Novelist and reformer Upton Sinclair born.

1879

Edison patents the incandescent lamp (lightbulb); George Washington Cable, *Old Creole Days;* Henry James, *Daisy Miller.*

1880

Henry Adams, *Democracy;* George Washington Cable, *The Grandissimes;* William Dean Howells, *The Undiscovered Country;* Lew Wallace's, *Ben Hur.*

1881

President James A. Garfield is assassinated; Henry James, *The Portrait of a Lady* and *Washington Square.*

1882

William Dean Howells, *A Modern Instance;* Mark Twain, *The Prince and the Pauper.*

1883

Brooklyn Bridge opens; first skyscraper built in Chicago; Mark Twain, *Life on the Mississippi.*

1884

Mark Twain, *Adventures of Huckleberry Finn.*

1885

William Dean Howells, *The Rise of Silas Lapham;* novelist Sinclair Lewis born.

1886

Karl Marx's *Das Kapital* available in English; William Dean Howells begins his "Editor's Study" series in *Harper's Monthly Magazine,* and publishes *Indian Summer;* Henry James, *The Bostonians;* Sarah Orne Jewett, *A White Heron.*

1887

William Dean Howells, *The Minister's Charge;* Mary Wilkins Freeman, *A Humble Romance and Other Stories.*

1888

Invention of the first electric motor and the first box camera; Edward Bellamy, *Looking Backward;* Henry James, *The Aspern Papers* and *Partial Portraits.*

1889

William Dean Howells, *Annie Kilburn;* Mark Twain, *A Connecticut Yankee in King Arthur's Court.*

1890

Passage of the Sherman Anti-Trust Act; William James, *The Principles of Psychology;* Jacob Riis, *How the Other Half Lives;* William Dean Howells, *A Hazard of New Fortunes.*

1891

Ambrose Bierce, *Tales of Soldiers and Civilians*; Mary Wilkins Freeman, *A New England Nun and Other Stories;* Hamlin Garland, *Main-Travelled Roads;* William Dean Howells, *Criticism and Fiction.*

1892

Violent strikes at Andrew Carnegie's steel company in Homestead, Pennsylvania; Charlotte Perkins Gilman, "The Yellow Wallpaper."

1893

Widespread financial panic leads to a serious economic depression; World's Columbian Exposition in Chicago; Stephen Crane, *Maggie: A Girl of the Streets.*

1894

Nationwide railway strike and extensive labor violence in Chicago; first motion picture is screened in New York; Kate Chopin, *Bayou Folk;* Hamlin Garland, *Crumbling Idols;* William Dean Howells, *A Traveller from Alturia;* Mark Twain, *The Tragedy of Pudd'nhead Wilson.*

1895

Invention of the radio by Marconi; Stephen Crane, *The Red Badge of Courage.*

1896

Paul Laurence Dunbar, *Lyrics of Lowly Life;* Harold Fredric, *The Damnation of Theron Ware;* Sarah Orne Jewett, *The Country of the Pointed Firs.*

1897

Henry James, *What Maisie Knew;* Edwin Arlington Robinson, *The Children of the Night.*

1898

Spanish-American War, April 25–August 12; Stephen Crane, *The Open Boat and Other Tales of Adventure;* Finley Peter Dunne, *Mr. Dooley in Peace and War.*

1899

Kate Chopin, *The Awakening;* Charles Chesnutt, *The Conjure Woman;* Henry James, *The Awkward Age;* Stephen Crane, *The Monster and Other Stories;* Frank Norris, *McTeague.*

1900

Death of Stephen Crane; Theodore Dreiser, *Sister Carrie;* Charles Chesnutt, *The House Behind the Cedars;* Jack London, *The Son of the Wolf;* Mark Twain, *The Man That Corrupted Hadleyburg;* Theodore Roosevelt, *The Strenuous Life.*

1901

President William McKinley assassinated shortly after his re-election and, succeeded by Theodore Roosevelt (1901–1909); Frank Norris, *The Octopus;* Charles Chesnutt, *The Marrow of Tradition;* Booker T. Washington, *Up from Slavery.*

1902

Death of Frank Norris; William James, *The Varieties of Religious Experience;* Owen Wister, *The Virginian;* Henry James, *The Wings of the Dove.*

1903

The Wright brothers make the first manned flight; Henry Ford founds the Ford Motor Company; W.E.B. Du Bois, *The Souls of Black Folk;* Henry James, *The Ambassadors;* Jack London, *The Call of the Wild;* Frank Norris, *The Pit* and *The Responsibilities of the Novelist,* published posthumously.

1904

Death of Kate Chopin; Henry Adams, *Mont-Saint-Michel and Chartres;* Henry James, *The Golden Bowl;* Jack London, *The Sea-Wolf;* publication of pioneering "muckraking" works of ex-posé journalism.

1905

Edith Wharton, *The House of Mirth.*

1906

Upton Sinclair, *The Jungle;* Mark Twain, *What Is Man?*

1907

Jack London, *The Iron Heel;* Henry Adams, *The Education of Henry Adams;* Henry James, *The American Scene;* William James *Pragmatism.*

1908

Henry Ford begins mass production of the Model T automobile; Jack London, *Martin Eden;* publication of pioneering works of the Modernist movement by Ezra Pound (*Personae)* and Gertrude Stein (*Three Lives*).

1910

Death of Mark Twain; Edwin Arlington Robinson, *The Town Down the River.*

1911

Supreme Court orders the breakup of Standard Oil Company and the American Tobacco Company due to their monopolistic practices; Theodore Dreiser, *Jennie Gerhardt;* Edith Wharton, *Ethan Frome.*

1912

Titanic sinks; Theodore Dreiser, *The Financier;* Zane Grey, *Riders of the Purple Sage;* James Weldon Johnson, *Autobiography of an Ex-Colored Man.*

1913

Willa Cather, *O Pioneers!;* Ellen Glasgow, *Virginia;* Edith Wharton, *The Custom of the Country;* Robert Frost, *A Boy's Will.*

1914

Opening of the Panama Canal; World War I begins in Europe; Theodore Dreiser, *The Titan;* Robert Frost, *North of Boston.*

1915

Willa Cather, *The Song of the Lark;* Theodore Dreiser, *The Genius;* Edgar Lee Masters, *Spoon River Anthology.*

1916

Death of Henry James; Robert Frost, *Mountain Interval;* Carl Sandburg, *Chicago Poems;* John Dewey, *Democracy and Education.*

1917

United States enters World War I; Hamlin Garland, *Son of the Middle Border;* T.S. Eliot publishes one of the first major poems of the Modernist movement, *The Love Song of J. Alfred Prufrock.*

1918

World War I ends; Willa Cather, *My Antonia.*

1919

Volstead Act introduces Prohibition; Sherwood Anderson, *Winesburg, Ohio.*

1920

Death of William Dean Howells; Sinclair Lewis, *Main Street;* Edith Wharton, *The Age of Innocence.*

FOR FURTHER RESEARCH

Lars Ahnebrink, *The Beginnings of Naturalism in American Fiction, 1891–1903.* Cambridge: Harvard University Press, 1950.

Erich Auerbach, *Mimesis: The Representation of Reality in Western Literature.* Princeton, NJ: Princeton University Press, 1953.

Michael Davitt Bell, *The Problem of American Realism: Studies in the Cultural History of a Literary Idea.* Chicago: University of Chicago Press, 1993.

Warner Berthoff, *The Ferment of Realism: American Literature, 1884–1919.* New York: Free Press, 1965.

Edwin H. Cady, *The Light of Common Day: Realism in American Fiction.* Bloomington: Indiana University Press, 1971.

Everett Carter, *Howells and the Age of Realism.* Philadelphia: Lippincott, 1954.

Richard Chase, *The American Novel and Its Tradition.* Garden City, NY: Doubleday Anchor, 1957.

Christophe Den Tandt, *The Urban Sublime in American Literary Naturalism.* Urbana: University of Illinois Press, 1998.

Lilian R. Furst, *All Is True: The Claims and Strategies of Realist Fiction.* Durham, NC: Duke University Press, 1995.

———, *Realism.* London: Longman, 1992.

June Howard, *Form and History in American Literary Naturalism.* Chapel Hill: University of North Carolina Press, 1985.

Howard Mumford Jones, *The Age of Energy: Varieties of American Experience, 1865–1914.* New York: Viking, 1971.

Amy Kaplan, *The Social Construction of American Realism.* Chicago: University of Chicago Press, 1988.

Alfred Kazin, *On Native Grounds: An Interpretation of Modern American Prose Literature.* New York: Reynal and Hitchcock, 1942.

Harold H. Kolb Jr., *The Illusion of Life: American Realism as a Literary Form.* Charlottesville: University Press of Virginia, 1969.

Maurice Larkin, *Man and Society in Nineteenth Century Realism, Determinism and Literature.* Totowa, NJ: Rowman and Littlefield, 1977.

Jay Martin, *Harvests of Change: American Literature 1865–1914.* Englewood Cliffs, NJ: Prentice-Hall, 1967.

Ronald E. Martin, *American Literature and the Universe of Force.* Durham, NC: Duke University Press, 1981.

Donald Pizer, *The Cambridge Companion to American Realism and Naturalism: Howells to London.* Cambridge: Cambridge University Press, 1995.

———, *Documents of American Realism and Naturalism.* Carbondale: Southern Illinois University Press, 1998.

———, *Realism and Naturalism in Nineteenth-Century American Literature.* Rev. Ed. Carbondale: Southern Illinois University Press, 1984.

———, *The Theory and Practice of American Literary Naturalism: Selected Essays and Reviews.* Carbondale: Southern Illinois University Press, 1984.

David E. Shi, *Facing Facts: Realism in American Thought and Culture, 1850–1920.* Oxford: Oxford University Press, 1995.

Eric J. Sundquist, ed., *American Realism: New Essays.* Baltimore, MD: Johns Hopkins University Press, 1982.

Alan Trachtenberg, *The Incorporation of America: Culture and Society in the Gilded Age.* New York: Hill and Wang, 1982.

Charles C. Walcutt, *American Literary Naturalism: The Divided Stream.* Minneapolis: University of Minnesota Press, 1956.

Larzer Ziff, *The American 1890s: Life and Times of a Lost Generation.* New York: Viking, 1966.

INDEX

George Bellows, *Cliff Dwellers*, 1913,
Los Angeles County Museum of Art.